There's No
Such Thing
as a
Comfortable Bra

There's No Such Thing as a Comfortable Bra

Sara Jane Coffman

SUNSTONE
PRESS

SANTA FE

Sunstone books may be purchased for educational, business, or sales promotional use.
For information please write: Special Markets Department, Sunstone Press,
P.O. Box 2321, Santa Fe, New Mexico 87504-2321.

Book and Cover design › Vicki Ahl
Body typeface › Bernhard Modern Std
Printed on acid-free paper

Library of Congress Cataloging-in-Publication Data

Coffman, Sara Jane.
 There's no such thing as a comfortable bra / by Sara Jane Coffman.
    pages cm
 ISBN 978-0-86534-930-8 (softcover : alk. paper)
 1. Women--Humor. 2. Brassieres--Humor. I. Title.
 PN6231.W6C646 2013
 818'.602--dc23

                                2012048944

WWW.SUNSTONEPRESS.COM
SUNSTONE PRESS / POST OFFICE BOX 2321 / SANTA FE, NM 87504-2321 /USA
(505) 988-4418 / ORDERS ONLY (800) 243-5644 / FAX (505) 988-1025

This book is dedicated to all those women
who, at least once in their lifetimes, found a bra that fit.
They give hope to the rest of us that some day we, too, might find one.

Contents

WHAT PRICE GLAMOUR?

There's No Such Thing as a Comfortable Bra . .9

My Straight, Flat Hair 16

This Won't Hurt a Bit 23

Ode to My Messy Closet. 26

Pilates: A Fairy Tale 27

LIFE'S LITTLE CHALLENGES

One of Those Days 29

College Students Next Door. 33

Cooking Disasters 37

I Just Wanted a Chair 42

How I'd Change the World 49

LOL WITH LOTS OF FRIENDS

An Afternoon with My Bridge Club 51

My Will 57

My Most Memorable Book Signing. 65

How to Enjoy Being Single 73

MEN

Driving Miss Sally. 78

Men in the Ladies' Room 82

Dating After Forty 84

Thank You Notes 88

Meeting Tom's Mother 89

Saying "Break a Leg" is not Enough 91

My Worst Blind Date 93

My Dad 97

LIGHTS, CAMERA, ACTION

Directing the Comedy Readers. 104

My Finest (and Not So Fine)

Moments in the Theatre 108

Shooting the Cover of My Book 118

Joining the Church Choir. ... ... .124

BRINGING HOME THE BACON

What I Like About My Job ... ... .129

Seeing My Book for the First Time. ... ... .133

My First Fan Letter.. ... ... .138

RELAX AND UNWIND

A Well-Deserved, Much-Needed Vacation 141

Should've Just Sent a Present.. ... ... .148

Las Vegas through the Eyes of a Midwesterner ..152

A Secret about Myself ... ... .158

WHAT PRICE GLAMOUR?

There's No Such Thing as a Comfortable Bra

It felt like I was having a heart attack. I was in the middle of a play at our local Civic Theatre when I felt a stabbing pain in my chest. I tried to ignore it, but it happened again—this time worse. A heart attack? I couldn't be having a heart attack. I was in the middle of a play.

As the pain continued, I tried to recall: was there a protocol for having a heart attack in the middle of a show? I considered my options. I could wait until the show was over, then drive myself to the emergency room. I could stop, sit down on the edge of the stage, and ask if there was an EMT in the audience. Or, I could simply raise my hand and ask the director—who was sitting in the audience—what to do.

Then it hit me.

My new bra was too tight.

Out of the millions of bras in the world, I have yet to find one that's comfortable. It's either too tight or too loose. When it's too tight, I can't breathe. When it's too loose, the straps fall down my shoulders. If it has hooks, the hooks dig into my back when I lean back in a chair. I'm also constantly readjusting the cups—up, down, left, right. When I get the cups where I want them, I have to readjust the straps.

My problems with bras began back in junior high. I didn't develop as quickly as the other girls did, so to keep up with them, I stuffed my bra with Kleenex. The pieces of Kleenex would shift, depending on how many times I raised my hand to answer the teachers' questions. So between classes, I'd run to the restroom and reposition them. If my classmates noticed that I changed shape—or was lopsided—from one class to the next, they were too polite (or mortified) to mention it.

The only thing worse than wearing a bra is shopping for one. Before you even get to the store, you have to decide: Do you want padded, or unpadded? Underwire or no underwire? Front-closing, back closing, or one-piece with no closing? Do you want thin straps, thick straps, or no straps? Do you want to spend half your paycheck, or your entire paycheck? And, most importantly, are you buying it for support, to create cleavage, or make it easy for your date to take off?

The other day my favorite bra disintegrated in the washing machine. I needed to buy a new one. They weren't making that style anymore (of course), so I had to start from scratch. After trying on approximately a hundred bras, and having no luck, I bought a pretzel at Mr. and Mrs. Pretzel and returned home.

A few days later, as I was surfing the web, I decided to type in "bras" to see what I'd find. There were thousands of hits. Cool. But if I bought a bra online, how would I know what size to order? Aha. They'd thought of that. The sites included videos on how to measure yourself. Oh-Kay.

I got my tape measure out of my sewing kit and sat down at my computer to watch the first video.

The formula was simple. You measured around your chest (below your breasts), and around the fullest part of your breasts. You then subtracted the smaller number from the larger, multiplied it by two, and took the square root of the hypotenuse. According to their chart, I took a size 38AA. Huh? Does anyone even make a size 38AA?

Then I watched the video from Bra Company #2. According to *their* formula, I needed a size 32DD. Huh? Does anyone even make a size 32DD?

I gave up on the Internet.

My friend Claire, who knew the trouble I was having, told me the only way to buy a bra was to get measured by an expert. So I went to the most upscale store at the mall, found a saleslady in the lingerie department, and told her I was looking for a comfortable bra. She whipped out her measuring tape and suggested we begin by finding my size. Instead of taking me into a dressing room, like Claire said she would, she measured me over my t-shirt—right there next to the cash register.

"Lift up your girls!" she said cheerfully.

I had no clue what she was talking about. I looked at her, clueless.

"Your girls!" she said, pointing at my chest.

My girls. Oh. Oh-Kay.

After taking the measurements, she proclaimed—to everyone within hearing distance—that I was a 36B. Young mothers pushing strollers and grandmothers holding up undergarments stopped what they were doing and gave me embarrassed little smiles. I gave them all back a little wave.

After trying on approximately one hundred size 36B bras (all too tight), I managed to slip away from the saleslady and go hunting on my own. Not only did nothing (of any size) fit, but the bras were extremely unflattering. If I was going to buy a bra that wasn't going to fit, I at least wanted it not to fit in lace or satin. As I sneaked out of the lingerie department, I threw a smile at the unfortunate woman getting measured by the saleslady next to the cash register.

Since I was already at the mall, I decided to try the store that specialized in lingerie that was polka dotted, striped, flowered, and fire engine red. I wasn't sure I wanted something polka dotted, striped, flowered, or fire engine red, but since I was there, I might as well try some on. As I was making my selections, the teen-aged girl working there followed me around the store and slipped them discretely into a fashionable bag so I wouldn't have to walk around holding the bras in my hot little hand.

Same story. When the bra fit my breasts, it was too tight around my chest. When it fit around my chest, the straps wouldn't stay up on my shoulders. Now I knew why, in history books, the Roman women always looked so lopsided. They were reaching under their togas to pull their bra strap up.

I bought a pretzel at Mr. and Mrs. Pretzel and returned home.

My friend Diane suggested I try a sports bra. According to her, sports bras provided the right amount of support and yet were made of material that stretched. That sounded promising. During my lunch hour the next day, I drove to a nearby sporting store, found a sports bra that looked about right, and went into the dressing room to try it on. I pulled it on over my head.

It fit. I liked it. It was comfortable. I liked the way I looked in it. I decided to buy it.

Then came the trouble: I couldn't get it off. Gravity got it on, but gravity was not going to get me out of it ... unless I stood on my head. Lunch hour was almost over. I had to get back to my office. I considered opening the dressing room door, sticking my head out, and asking the clerk in the treadmill department to come in and pull it off for me.

Eventually I devised a system. With my left hand, I pulled the right strap up and extracted my right arm, starting with my elbow. The bra was now cutting off the blood flow to my carotid artery. Knowing I had just a few moments of air left, I reversed the process. With my right hand, I raised the left strap up and freed my left arm and shoulder. Then, with one last, final burst of adrenaline, I pulled the bra off over my head.

I sat down to catch my breath. Who would buy such a contraption? A contortionist?

Meanwhile, my significant other, Sam, came across an ad for a bra in the local paper. It had the same features of a sports bra (no hooks), but was made out of a light, airy material. And it was only $6.95. How could I go wrong at $6.95? I went out on a limb and ordered two.

They were perfect!

Until I washed them.

After I washed them, the elastic around my chest still fit, but the material covering my breasts had stretched. My breasts hung down like two slinkies.

Was I the only woman in the world who had trouble finding a bra? I was ready to walk into grocery stores, movie theatres, and restaurants and yell: "Is anyone here wearing a comfortable bra?"

Before I went that far, I surveyed my closest friends. Did any of *them* own a comfortable bra?

They all had stories to tell. Take my friend Betty in Colorado Springs, Colorado.

Because of the size of her "girls," Betty said she buys expensive "front loading" bras that offer maximum support. But once, on vacation in Maine, she packed only her cheaper bras. While she was sitting on a rock overlooking the ocean, she was engulfed by a large wave. Her bra, consisting of material obviously not up to the task, instantly became size FF, with her breasts hanging down to her waist.

Two of my friends in Lafayette, Indiana—Linda and M.J.—both said they hate their bras so much that they take them off the minute they get home. Well, M.J. does. Linda takes hers off as soon as she gets in the car—while she's driving. You're probably familiar with the method she uses—she unhooks the hooks, pulls the straps down off her shoulders, then extracts the bra through her sleeve. (Linda wanted me to add that she carries a sweatshirt in the car to put on if she has to stop at McDonald's to go to the bathroom. Oh-Kay.)

My friend Diane in Winston-Salem, North Carolina, wears a sports bra. She gets in and out of it by pulling it over her hips. (She's a size two.)

My friend Pat in Chicago tells of the time her front-closing bra flew open in the middle of a presentation. Standing at the head of a conference table addressing an all-male audience, she gestured a bit too enthusiastically. Understandingly, she never again wore a front-closing bra.

My eighty-year-old friend Jeanne in Malvern, Pennsylvania, tells of the time she took several bras into the dressing room to try them on. A short time later, the saleslady knocked on the door and stuck her head in to see if she could help. She asked Jeanne if she was pregnant.

"Pregnant?" Jeanne laughed. "I'm eighty!"

"Well, two of the bras you brought in are nursing bras."

And, of course, we've all seen the unfortunate wardrobe malfunctions that occur occasionally in the theatre, on TV, and in real life where things pop out unexpectedly. The owner, sometimes fazed and sometimes unfazed—pops them back in and continues on.

Men aren't any more comfortable with bras than women are. Years ago, I was at the bank signing papers to buy my house. My banker, my attorney, and my real estate agent (all men) were sitting with me at the table. When it was time to sign the papers, I reached into the pocket of my blazer to get a pen. Along with the pen, out came the sexy black bra I'd been wearing the night before.

The men diverted their eyes while I stuffed it back into my pocket. They were much more embarrassed than I was. I wished they'd laughed so I could have, too.

As of writing this story, I continue my quest to find a comfortable bra.

If I don't find one soon, I'm thinking about taking one of my old bras and just stuffing it with Kleenex.

My Straight, Flat Hair

This is a chapter about the problems I've had with my hair and my observations about hair in general. If you're one of those fortunate people who's happy with your hair, you can skip this chapter and go on to the next one.

First of all, here's my theory about how I got such lousy hair. I think that before we're born, we have to stand in line for some of the traits we're going to be born with. There are a limited number of some of the traits that are handed out. In my case, I was near the front of the line for such things as "intelligence" and "sense of humor," but in the back of the line for "great hair." They'd finished passing out all the "great hair" by the time I got to the front of the line.

So, my hair is thin, fine, straight, and flat. In case you're not familiar with the terminology (I wasn't either), "thin" refers to the number of hairs per square inch. I have very few. "Fine" refers to the diameter of each individual hair shaft. Mine are skinny. "Straight" is the opposite of curly. And "flat" means that even on a good day I look like Alfalfa in the Little Rascals.

Starting from when I was around age two, my mother (who'd been a hairdresser before she got married and who may have wanted to keep up her hairdressing skills in case things didn't work out with my dad) gave me home perms. She was probably trying to give my hair some "body," but the perms never took. Besides, they made my hair smell so bad, the rest of the family wouldn't come near me for days.

When I was in junior high, the hair color "Nice and Easy" came out. It promised to make hair sexy and shiny. I nagged my mother to let me try it but always got the same response—"Not in my lifetime,"

"Not while you're living under my roof," or "Over my dead body." I can't remember her exact words, but that was the sentiment. So, I did what any teenager would do. I bought a box of "Nice and Easy," sneaked into the bathroom when my mother wasn't home, and colored my hair.

It came out about three shades darker than my regular color, but I was convinced that the only thing people would notice was how sexy and shiny my hair was.

At dinner that night, my mother asked me if I'd colored my hair.

"You told me I couldn't," I said truthfully. From behind her back, she pulled out the towel I'd used—covered with big, black stains from the dye.

Oh. That.

In high school, I went for volume instead of color. I teased my hair up on top of my head as high as I could, secured it with a ton of Aqua Net Hair Spray, then pinned a curly hairpiece to the back. That worked fine until I went to college.

Along with the other freshmen in my dorm, I wanted desperately to pledge a sorority. I remember the Saturday we were all invited to the sorority we really wanted to join. We got off the bus in front of the sorority house and waited to be invited in. Disaster struck. A big wind came up and blew my hairpiece off. It rolled down the middle of the street, with me chasing it in my high heeled shoes. Too embarrassed to excuse myself to go to the ladies room and pin it back on, I held it in my lap during my interviews.

I wasn't asked to join that sorority—or any other.

I'm sure it had nothing to do with my hairpiece blowing off.

I doubt that it had anything to do with my hairpiece blowing off.

Well, it may have. I'll never know.

Before you get the wrong idea, I should explain that, at times, my hair looks good. If I use *exactly* the right amount of *precisely* the right kind of shampoo, curl my hair with a curling iron for ten seconds per curl, use *exactly* the right amount of *precisely* the right kind of hairspray, and the moon is in the seventh power, my hair looks good. Of course, that's only if I stay indoors. If I go outside, all bets are off.

On the days I don't have time to do my hair, I wear a hat. I'm not the only person who's ever thought of this—throughout history, people have worn hats to cover up their hair. Knights wore helmets, not to protect themselves on the battlefield. They were having bad hair days. Women wore bonnets, not to look more fashionable. They were having bad hair days. And why do young people wear baseball caps? I repeat: they're having bad hair days.

My hat collection resides on the top shelf in my hall closet. You probably have the same shelf in your hall closet. When you throw a hat up there, the whole pile comes crashing down on your head and you have to stop what you're doing and pick them all up.

My pile consists of:

An assortment of various baseball hats of different sizes and
colors—all having seen better days,
A Russian fur hat with flaps,
A bicycle helmet I'm keeping, even though I'll never use it again,
A head scarf in case I ever get cast as Yentl,
A pair of semi-chewed earmuffs that Linda's dog Bruiser got hold
of the last time I babysat. I had no idea a 130-pound golden
Labrador retriever could reach up and snatch something from
the middle of a dining room table,
A cardboard Burger King crown that I might use for a birthday
party someday,

A collection of detachable hoods from my winter coats that I take off because they're bulky and they push me forward when I'm driving so my face ends up smashed against the steering wheel,

A stocking cap I bought from a street vendor in San Francisco because I thought San Francisco would be warm, but it's not, and the people in San Francisco don't tell you that ahead of time because they want you to buy sweatshirts and hats from them,

A white sunhat with a big brim,

One of my dad's brown fedoras from the fifties,

An old-fashioned rain hat that folds up so I can put it in my purse, and finally,

A cowboy hat with three arrows stuck through it that I made for a workshop I did to show faculty what could happen to them if they gave a bad lecture.

Much as I'd like to wear a hat on a daily basis, it's just not practical. Which brings me to the most important thing you must do when you have fine hair—get a good haircut.

My stylist is Scotty. Every time she cuts my hair, she reminds me that her scissors cost $300.00. She reminds me because sometimes I cut my hair myself. I don't set out to cut my hair—it just happens.

Here's how. I'll be sitting watching TV and start playing with my hair. I'll find a few hairs that seem longer than the others, so, during the commercial, I get out my sewing scissors (which do *not* cost $300.00) that I keep in a tackle box with all my sewing stuff on the top shelf in my hall closet (next to my hats). I cut the longer strands off. I return the scissors to my tackle box and put it back on the shelf in the closet.

I return to my program.

Pretty soon, I find a spot on the opposite side of my head that needs trimmed (to match the side I've already cut). So I get the scissors back out and trim those, promising myself that the first thing the next morning I'll call Scotty for an appointment. Scotty knows what she's doing. And Scotty's scissors cost $300.00.

During the next commercial, I go to the basement and hide the tackle box in the far corner on a shelf that I can only reach by standing on a folding lawn chair. I return to my program. And immediately start playing with my hair again. This time I find a piece that's REALLY sticking out. Even Scotty would tell me to go ahead and trim it. I go down to the basement, retrieve my scissors and trim that little sliver of hair. Note: no longer am I trimming my hair just during the commercials. Now I'm trimming it during the program.

I know I shouldn't cut my own hair, but I can't help it. I'm either a frustrated hairdresser, or just plain frustrated.

At least when I go to Scotty, I don't try to hide the fact that I've been cutting my hair myself. I tell her right up front.

"No kidding," she'll say, rolling her eyes.

The last time I was in, she questioned me about what part of my hair I cut. I told her I cut the little ends off to make the row of hair even.

"Don't do that," she explained. "I make them uneven for a reason. That way the shorter hairs support the longer hairs and make your hair fluffy."

Oh.

My many hair disasters have led me to create a list of hair "truisms," such as:

1. If your mother and grandmother had thin, straight hair, you will too.

2. People who have straight hair want curly hair. And vise versa.

3. If you discover you used the wrong setting on your do-it-yourself hair clippers after the first swipe of your hair, you'll very likely need to use that same setting for the remainder of your hair.

4. Coloring your hair yourself is not going to correct the bad perm you gave yourself.

5. The likelihood of your coming out of the beauty shop with a hairdo that even remotely resembles the picture you've brought in is nil. Of course, the likelihood that you're the same age as the model in the picture is also nil.

6. You will always like the way your stylist does your hair better on the days when you're not going someplace important than on the days when you plan to attend your ex-boyfriend's wedding.

7. On the one day that you're in a hurry, your hair stylist will be running late.

8. When you've had a certain hairstyle for a while, and your boyfriend (husband or significant other) has never complimented you on it, he'll be sure to tell you that he liked the old way better if you go and change it.

9. On the day that your beauty salon's hot water heater gives up the ghost, your stylist won't remember to tell you until after she's colored your hair and then has to rinse it for ten minutes ... in cold water.

10. You need to be specific when you ask your stylist to cut your hair. I once asked my stylist to "just trim off the split ends." The next thing I knew there was a six inch piece of hair in my lap. I left the salon with a pixie cut feeling like a stack of shredded wheat with glasses.

11. When a hair stylist leans you back to wash your hair and sees that your head is nowhere near the basin, don't let her pull on your neck to get it there.

12. When you finally find a hair stylist you like, she won't be there the next time you go in. She'll have moved to another state.

I know there are a lot worse things in life than having thin hair. The one thing that keeps me going, though, is the hope that I'm going to have great hair when I get to heaven. I want lots of thick, dark, curly hair. I want enough hair to be able to wear pigtails (like Abby on NCIS), or to pull it back into a ponytail. I want such beautiful hair that the angels are going to fight over whose turn it is to braid it.

But recently I read the book *90 Minutes in Heaven* and I've begun to worry about my "great hair in heaven" theory. The book tells the story about a man who's in a serious car accident. At the scene of the accident, the paramedics pronounce him dead. In the book, though, the author describes going to heaven. And ninety minutes later—according to the paramedics—he came back to life.

I don't have any trouble believing that he went to heaven, but here's my problem. He writes: "the first person I recognized was my grandfather. He looked exactly as I remembered him, with his shock of white hair."

Shoot. Does that mean I'm going to have straight hair in heaven?

This Won't Hurt a Bit

The other day I asked my dermatologist about a problem I was having with my complexion. Sun damage, he said. He recommended some quick laser surgery. "Quick" and "surgery" didn't quite seem to go together in the same sentence, but I thought about it for a while and decided to have it done.

My appointment was at 9:50. When I arrived, the nurse took me into a room with a fancy chair. Good sign—the doctor must be running on time. I stretched out in the fancy chair and started my deep breathing. Having had acupuncture in the past, I knew that if I relaxed, I didn't notice the needles going in. I'd also read that when you have adrenaline pumping through your system (which happens when you're scared), it slows down the healing process. So I was going to relax, and stay relaxed.

The chair was comfortable so it was easy to go to my happy place. I was almost asleep when a nurse came in, apologized, and asked me to move to the room next door. They needed my room for a quick laser treatment. Sure. I collected my things (jacket, winter gloves, sunglasses, bottle of cleanser I'd brought to ask the doctor about, car keys, and my little purse). The gloves, sunglasses, bottle of cleanser, and car keys fell to the floor and the nurse bent down and helped me pick them up. I'd recently bought a cute little purse and the gloves, sunglasses, car keys, and bottle of cleanser didn't fit inside.

The second room wasn't quite as comfortable as the first. The chairs were hard and the room wasn't soundproof. I could hear the nurse preparing the patient. Something about goggles. Something about bright lights. I didn't particularly want to know what I was in for, so I moved to a chair farther from the door and began my deep breathing again. Again, I went to my happy place. I was almost asleep when a different nurse came in and said they were ready for me. I collected my stuff again (keys, jacket, gloves, bottle of cleanser, purse, and sunglasses) and moved back to the first room.

I stretched out in the fancy chair and started deep breathing again.

I was almost asleep when a different nurse came in, apologized, and asked me to move to the room next door. Once again, I collected all my stuff and moved back to the little waiting room. I didn't feel like going to my happy place again, so I tried to keep my mind busy in other ways.

I went through my entire exercise workout routine in my head. Then, for real, I did my stretches sitting there in the chair. I tried to recall all of the names of the kids in my first grade class. I made a list of the things I needed at the grocery store. I planned all my meals for the next month. Then I ran out of things to think about. There was no sign of the doctor. Or the nurses. I was getting hungry. So I did the unthinkable.

I opened the door and went out into the hallway.

At the far end, I could see a nurse on the phone. Before I knew it, one of the receptionists from the front desk appeared and asked if she could help me. I said I was wondering if maybe the building was on fire and everyone had left without telling me. She said she'd find someone right away.

In came Lisa, one of Dr. Richards' assistants. She explained that Dr. Richards was in surgery. (What was I? Chopped liver?)

I'd heard good things about Lisa, so I asked her if she'd do the procedure. She'd be glad to. Again, I started my deep breathing. Lisa handed me a pair of goggles to cover my eyes, then said: "It's going to feel like I'm hitting you with a rubber band."

Okay. I could deal with that.

"I'll try it once so you can see what it feels like."

She zapped me. There were bright fireworks of light. I flew across the room and hit the back wall. Crawling on my hands and knees, I pulled myself back into the chair. What the heck kind of rubber band had she been talking about? She zapped me again. This time I flew up and hit my head on the ceiling. The nurse assisting Lisa grabbed hold of my ankles and pulled me back down into the chair. Lisa continued zapping.

That's when I smelled the burning flesh. My flesh.

I began saying to myself: "I'm glad I'm doing this, but I am never going to do this again." "I'm glad I'm getting this done, but I am never going to have this done again."

Seventeen zaps later, Lisa told the nurse she was changing the size of the laser in order to do the spots on my nose. That couldn't be good. With my luck, she was not going from a larger laser to a smaller one.

Six zaps later, I was done. I was glad I did it, but I was never going to have it done again.

On my way out, Lisa told me to stop by the front desk and make an appointment to come back in a month.

"For a checkup?" I asked.

"No, for another treatment. Dr. Richards *did* explain this procedure needs to be done three times, didn't he?"

Ode to My Messy Closet

A Poemette
by
Sara Jane Coffman

When I was in Nova Scotia
I bought
the most beautiful,
soft,
fuzzy,
warm,
blue tartan
plaid scarf
to wear with my winter coat.
It's in my closet.

Somewhere.

Pilates: A Fairy Tale

Once upon a time there was a beautiful, middle-aged princess who had a great sense of adventure. One day, in her quest for a *new* adventure, she decided to take a Pilates class.

Believing there would only be other middle-aged princesses in the class, she was surprised to find it was comprised of young females with superhuman powers. The princess noticed that the young females with superhuman powers wore matching outfits (and sweatbands) and carried matching exercise mats. The princess, wearing her old sweats, bravely unrolled her (borrowed) exercise mat and took a spot on the floor in the middle of the room.

The instructor began by having everyone bend forward and touch their toes. She looked over at the beautiful middle-aged princess and said:

"Or, your ankles."

She looked over at the middle-aged princess again, and said: "Or, your knees."

Much as she tried, the middle-aged princess could not keep up with the superhuman females. She was only able to do one squat, crunch, and leg lift for every ten squats, crunches, and leg lifts the superhuman females were doing.

She had trouble keeping up in other ways as well.

Her borrowed exercise mat kept sliding around on the floor, so she had to stop and reposition it. Her exercise ball kept popping out and rolling away when she squeezed it between her knees. She spent a good bit of time chasing her ball. When she needed a drink of water, she had to stop and go to the drinking fountain far, far away, on the other side of the room. The superhuman females had their own (matching) water bottles to drink from.

For thirty minutes, the beautiful, middle-aged princess crunched, squatted, leg lifted, repositioned her mat, chased her ball, and went for water at the drinking fountain far, far away on the other side of the room. It was the hardest exercise class she'd ever taken. She was tired. And sore. She wanted to go home. Or to the mall.

The class finally ended. While the other students chatted on their way out, she lay prone on the floor and tried to recover.

One of the superhuman females approached her.

To congratulate her for completing the class? No. She whispered into the princess's ear: "If you put the rubber side of your mat face down, it won't slide all over the floor." Then she disappeared with all the others.

Using the last bit of effort she had, the beautiful middle-aged princess slowly got up and began rolling up her (borrowed) exercise mat.

The superhuman instructor looked over at her and said:

"You're not leaving, are you? This is just the break."

LIFE'S LITTLE CHALLENGES

One of Those Days

It was one of those days that started off badly, and then got worse.

To begin with, I hadn't slept well. During the night, my air conditioner had conked out and the house was miserably hot. So, the first thing I did when I got up was call the air conditioning people. They said they'd send someone over that afternoon to check it out.

To raise my spirits, I decided to wear my expensive, new navy blue slacks. The ones I'd brought home from the store, hemmed (because they were too long), and then washed. This obviously wasn't the right order to do those things in, because the slacks—which looked great in the store—were now about four inches too short.

Wonderful.

I was already running late. If I took the time to change my pants, I'd have to change everything else. I ran through my day in my head. Did I have any important appointments or meetings? No. I was just going to be sitting at my computer all day. So, instead of changing, I left for work in pants that were too short.

It wasn't until I was in the car that I remembered. Today was the day my boss was going to give a VIP from another campus a tour of our offices. Shoot. Oh, well. She always just stuck her head in my doorway, introduced me quickly, and moved on to David's office next door. All I was going to have to do was say "hello" and flash a big smile.

And that's exactly what happened. I was at my desk and heard her coming down the hall, stopping at every door and introducing the visitor to our staff. I straightened up the papers on my desk so they'd be perfectly vertical and perpendicular, and tried to look busy. When they arrived at my door, I flashed my smile and gave my cheerful "hello."

To my dismay, the visitor held out his hand. He stood in my doorway and held out his hand! Why would he do that? Now I was going to have to get up, walk around my desk, and go to the door. So I did what any professional woman would do. I got out of my chair, bent down four inches, then squatted to the door so my pants would look long enough.

The rest of the morning was uneventful.

During my lunch hour, I had an appointment at my eye doctor's to have a visual field test done. I'd never had one before, but the nurse assured me there was nothing to it. She began by having me rest my chin inside a machine. There was a screen I was supposed to look at, one eye at a time. She covered my other eye with a patch. Then she gave me a clicker (like a remote control) and instructed me to click the clicker whenever I saw a tiny dot on the screen.

It was a timed test. Was I ready? Sure. See a dot on the screen. Click the clicker. How hard could that be?

Immediately after the test began, I realized that my clicker was defective. I'd see a dot and hit the button, but the sound didn't register in the machine for several seconds after that. I wasn't able to tell the nurse my problem because my head was inside a machine ... and the test was being timed. So I sat there furiously clicking the clicker trying to catch up with the dots.

Besides dealing with a broken clicker, my brain was giving me fits. It couldn't decide whether or not I'd seen a dot. My eyes would see the dot and send the image to my brain, and then my brain would take its time: Was that a dot? It looked like a dot. Maybe it was a piece of lint. It could have been a piece of lint. Let's blink and see if we still see it. Well, that was dumb. Of course we're not going to see it. It was only on the screen for a second. Maybe we should just go ahead and call it a dot whether it was a dot or not. Okay. Go ahead. Tell the thumb to click the clicker.

Figuring I was going to fail the test, I just clicked the clicker every so often whether I saw a dot or not.

When the test was over, I waited for the doctor to come and give me my results. Good news. I'd seen enough dots to pass.

Returning to work, I managed to finish the day without any further crises. I was looking forward to going home and having a relaxing evening. In my air conditioned house. Then I remembered. I didn't have an air conditioned house. Sam and the air conditioning guy might still be there. (Sam had gone over to let him in.)

Indeed, when I got home, the two men were in the kitchen, sweat pouring down their faces, into puddles on the floor. And the kitchen was hot. Very hot. Even hotter than when I'd left that morning.

"How's it going?" I asked cheerfully.

They stared down at their feet.

I tried again: "Are you finished? Am I in time to write you a check?"

No answer.

I tried again: "How much do I owe you?

They kept looking at their feet. They still didn't speak.

I sensed doom.

Then they both started talking at once.

"There's not enough Freon in your system."

"You only have five pounds."

"You should have fifteen pounds."

"We tried to find the leak, but we couldn't."

"So you need a new coil."

"New coils cost almost half of what new units cost."

"You should consider replacing the whole unit."

"The life expectancy of an air conditioner is seventeen years."

"Yours is over twenty-one."

"If you want a new unit, you'll have to decide how much money you want to spend. We have all kinds. Oh. I've looked over your house and you're going to need another supply duct in the living room. And at least two more return ducts."

Huh? Supply ducts? Return ducts? Wouldn't it make sense if he didn't install a new supply duct, I wouldn't need a new return duct?

"Why do I need new ducts?" I asked.

"Oh, Ms. Coffman, we can't guarantee our work unless we put the new ducts in. By the way, this service call is one hundred and fifty dollars. And it can't be deducted from the cost of a new unit."

They stared at me again.

"So, what do you want to do?"

There I stood. In my kitchen. In my short pants. With sweat pouring down my face, into a puddle on the floor.

I reached for my checkbook. Hopefully, after I paid for a new air conditioner (and the service call), there'd be enough money left over to buy a new pair of pants.

College Students Next Door

The worst thing that could happen to a homeowner happened to me.

Two college students moved into the house next door.

As they were unloading their stereos, speakers, and large screen TVs from their big orange U-Haul trailer, I went over and introduced myself. I asked the neighborly questions:

"Where are you from?"

"What are your majors?" and

"What year in school are you?" What I really wanted to ask was:

"How much beer do you consume in a week?"

"Do you know to throw your beer cans in the recyclable container the city gives you and not in my front yard?"

"Are you planning on having any large parties?"

"How loud do you play your stereo?"

"Do you have any misdemeanors or felonies? Have you ever been arrested?"

"Do you do drugs?"

"What time do you typically go to bed? *Do* you go to bed?"

"Are you at all curious about what time *I* go to bed?"

"Could I have your parents' phone numbers so I can wake them up at two in the morning should you ever wake me up at that hour?"

Come to find out, both young men were majoring in engineering. That was good. Very good. They'd have to study to stay in engineering.

As I left, I gave my little "this will be a wonderful place for you to study because it's such a quiet neighborhood" speech, with particular emphasis on the word "quiet." If all went well, I'd never see them again.

All went well until the next night. I'd been asleep for about two hours when I awoke to the sound of a base drum. Boom. Boom. Boom. I got up and shut my bedroom window. Crawled back in bed and tried to go back to sleep. Boom. Boom. Boom. I pulled a pillow over my head. Boom. Boom. Boom. This was their first night in their new house. I'd cut them some slack. I turned the light on and read for a while. It was 12:30. Surely they'd go to bed soon.

Boom. Boom. Boom.

One a.m. Still booming.

One thirty. Still booming.

I had to go to work in the morning. I considered my options. I could call the police, but if the police came and the music had stopped by the time they arrived, I'd look like an idiot. Or, I could go over and ask them to turn their music down.

Which should it be? The police? Pay a visit myself? Police? Pay a visit myself? I decided to get dressed and pay a visit myself.

First, I had to decide: what is the appropriate attire to go over and talk to your neighbors at 1:30 in the morning? Should I put on makeup? Do my hair? I looked in the mirror. My hair was sticking out in all different directions. I decided to go "as is"—the lunatic next door neighbor. Putting my raincoat on over my nightgown, I pulled on my winter boots. It was summer, but I couldn't find my shoes, and I didn't want to go in my slippers.

Carrying my large, black police flashlight, I turned on my front porch light and stumbled my way across my dark yard. I knocked on their door, and, as politely as I could, asked the guys to turn their music down. They apologized profusely and immediately turned it down.

I went back to bed.

About a week or so later, as I left for work, I looked out my car window and noticed that the front of my house looked funny. I couldn't put my finger on it. That night, coming home, I looked again. Something wasn't right, but I couldn't say what. That went on for several days. Every time I drove past the house, I tried to figure out what was different. Something was different. What?

Then it hit me! The blue window box under my living room window was gone! Gone! Someone had taken it!

Who would steal my window box? I'd heard of people vandalizing mailboxes. But a window box? That was attached to my house? Who would do that?

My new neighbors? Surely not my new neighbors. They were friendly. Weren't they? Nobody would steal a window box. Would they? The more I thought about it, the madder I got. It had to be the boys next door.

What was this world coming to? Why can't young people respect their elders? I'd lived in my house for almost 30 years. It was my home. They were just transients. What made them think they were better than me? This is what happens when you have renters in a well-established neighborhood. I could have predicted this. And vandals of all things. No one has the right to destroy someone else's property.

I had two choices. I could either go over and talk to them about my window box ... or this time I could call the police. I decided to call the police.

Before I called, a little voice in my head told me to get out of the car, walk over to the large window, and investigate. When I got up to the bushes, I stopped. There was my window box. Lying on the ground between my bushes and the house. It was so old; it had completely disintegrated and fallen off the house.

Oh.

Oops.

I'm really rather glad I didn't call the police.

Excuse me. I'm going inside now to bake some cookies for the boys next door.

Cooking Disasters

I've mastered a lot of skills in my life. Cooking's not one of them.

My traumatic experiences with cooking began at an early age. When I was nine, my best friend Vicki came over to spend the night. To make the event really special, my mother gave us permission to use her special Betty Crocker waffle iron to make waffles for everyone in the morning. I'd watched her make waffles many times, but had never made them by myself.

Vicki and I were excited. We were going to make waffles for the whole family! By ourselves! And use the special Betty Crocker waffle iron!

The first thing in the morning, when everyone else was still asleep, we tiptoed down to the kitchen in our P.J.s and got started. My mother had set out all of the ingredients. All we had to do was mix everything together in the big yellow bowl. Which we did. But there was a bottle of something left over. We knew it had something to do with waffles. Huh. We looked at each other, and then proceeded to add some to the mixture. That looked promising. We decided to add even more. We added about half the bottle.

We poured the mixture into the waffle iron.

As the waffles heated up, the maple syrup turned to glue and stuck the two sides of waffle iron together. Oops.

We had corn flakes, instead of waffles, that morning for breakfast.

Then there was the time I made whipped cream. I must have done something wrong because it hardened into a lump that wouldn't come out of the bowl. Everyone was teasing me about it, so my granddad, who was visiting, came to my defense. He said he'd like to have some for his coffee. Using a steak knife, he chipped a piece out of the bowl, and dropped it into his steaming hot coffee. It floated around, but never did melt.

Then there was the time in high school when I offered my date one of the brownies I'd made for him. With his first bite, one of his teeth broke off. My dad drove him home so his parents could take him for an emergency visit to his dentist to get it glued back on.

Then there was the time my mother asked me to frost a cake. Instead of using powdered sugar I used granulated sugar. Big mistake. I can still remember my family sitting around the dinner table crunching our way through that gritty frosting. My parents, who grew up in the depression, didn't believe in wasting things, so they wouldn't throw the cake away. It took us forever to finish it off.

Cooking can be especially stressful over the holidays. I remember the year it was our family's turn to host Thanksgiving. While my mother was busy in the kitchen with the turkey, she sent me to the basement (where we had a mini-kitchen) with a box of instant potatoes. I was to make instant potatoes for twenty-five people. I followed the recipe *exactly*. They came out too dense. I ran upstairs and asked my mom what to do. With her arm inside the turkey, and everyone else running around like crazy, she told me to add more milk. I ran downstairs and added more milk. Then they were too runny. I ran upstairs again. With her head in the oven, she said to add more potato mix. I did. That went on all morning. Everyone was well into dessert by the time I finished the potatoes.

We never again used instant potatoes.

Nor was I ever again asked to help with Thanksgiving dinner.

Actually, it's my mother's fault that I can't cook. She rarely cooked. When I was growing up, my dad traveled a lot. He often left on Monday morning and didn't return until dinner on Friday night. When my dad was out-of-town, my mom heated up frozen pot pies. She had us convinced that pot pies were really special. Plus, she let us eat them in the living room in front of the TV set. Who wouldn't want to watch Roy Rogers or The Mickey Mouse Club—with a pot pie—in the living room?

On weekends, my mom *would* cook and we kids would try to act like it was normal to eat at the kitchen table with a complete set of silverware instead of with just a fork. (I don't think my dad ever knew about the pot pies.)

As an adult, I still struggle with cooking. Recently, I invited some friends over for dinner. I decided to make something safe. Something I'd made a number of times. Something you can't mess up. Chili. I carefully browned the best grade of ground beef I could get, then carefully sautéed the onion and green pepper in the juice. I added the tomatoes and the beans. I added the seasoning. I tasted it. It was perfect.

Then I screwed up. I was supposed to turn the heat down and let the chili simmer for thirty minutes. But I forgot. I went into the living room and started cleaning the house. The next thing I knew I smelled something burning.

I rushed back to the kitchen and discovered the bottom layer of chili—which was black—was stuck to the bottom of the pan. Worried about ruining my pan, I furiously began scraping the burned chili from the bottom. Little black flecks came loose and got mixed into the chili. Worried now about the chili, I furiously began to spoon the black flakes out of the chili into the sink. By the time my guests arrived, there was almost no chili left. I ordered out for pizza.

Sam can't cook any better than I can. One year, he announced he was having Thanksgiving at his house. He said he'd prepare the turkey and he assigned everyone in his family different side dishes to bring. His daughter-in-law was going to "take over" whatever was left to do to the turkey when she arrived on Thanksgiving Day.

Thanksgiving arrived. Everyone showed up promptly at noon with their hot dishes except for the daughter-in-law who sent word she had the flu.

Fortunately, HER mother, who we'd never met before, offered to help with the turkey. Had Sam started cooking it yet? No. She took off her linen blazer, rolled up the sleeves of her silk blouse, and asked to see it.

It was in the refrigerator.

Still frozen.

We ate ten hours later.

My friend Amy can't cook either. She once had trouble baking a store-bought pie. The directions said to put the pie on a cookie sheet (which she did) and bake it at 350 degrees, for an hour. When the hour was up, she peaked in. The pie crust was golden brown—it looked terrific.

But instead of pulling the pie out of the oven on the cookie sheet (like she should have), she tried to lift it by holding onto the edges of the aluminum pan. The tin buckled in half dumping the pie on the oven door. After letting loose a few expletives, she grabbed a spatula and scooped the hot, gooey, mess into a dish. She went ahead and ate it.

She called it apple "dump" pie.

Even good cooks have disasters. My friend Terri bought a large, disposable aluminum pan for her Thanksgiving turkey so she could just throw it away. Unfortunately, and unbeknownst to her, the aluminum pan she bought was not the highest quality. It sprung a hole in the bottom, and every time she pulled the turkey out to baste it, the hole got bigger. The drippings leaked from the pan onto the floor of the oven, and the kitchen filled up with smoke.

She had to open the doors and windows to get rid of the smoke.

She couldn't finish cooking anything in the oven—that would have produced even more smoke. So everyone put their winter coats on and ate their meal—turkey and cold casseroles—while staring longingly at the frozen pumpkin pie which was going to be for dessert.

Happily, cooking is no longer an issue for me. I figured it out. When my friends have a carry-in dinner, I offer to bring the wine. I buy the best, most expensive wine I can afford. It's worth every penny. I'm grateful that I don't have to cook, and everyone else is grateful that they don't have to eat anything I've made.

I Just Wanted a Chair

I'm always looking for ways to improve my writing. I'm especially curious about other writers. What are their secrets? How do they get their inspiration? One day, I heard an interview with an author who said she had a special chair she sat in when she wrote.

I should have a special chair, I thought.

So I went to the big furniture store. I found it right off the bat. It was a darling little "platform" rocker that rocked straight forward and straight backward. It came with a separate footstool that also rocked straight forward and straight backward. The blue-flowered cushions made it cottage-y, so it would fit in with the other cottage-style furniture in my house.

On my way to find a salesman, I tried sitting in one of the big recliners. Oh. It was nice. It was very nice. It had large, padded arms where I could lay my notes while I was working on my manuscript. It rocked. There was a bar on the side of the chair you could push down to make a footrest come up. Oh. That was nice. Very nice. My cats would like the footrest. So I started looking at recliners.

Then I saw it. Across the room. A gold velvet recliner that looked like a throne. It had piping around the seat cushion, and ten delicate little pleats in the back of the chair. The top of the chair didn't go across in a straight line, like all the other ones did—it had an elegant little arch. It was the perfect chair to write a book in.

I had to have it.

It was delivered later that week. It fit perfectly in the space at the foot of my bed in my upstairs where I was going to have my special writing corner. I'd never had such a beautiful piece of furniture. Now, I could sit and write my book.

But the first time I sat in the chair, I noticed how faded and threadbare the old cotton quilt on my bed was. After a few days, I realized I was either going to have to return the chair or buy a new bedspread.

That weekend, I visited my friend Diane in Winston-Salem and told her my dilemma. Return the chair, or buy a fancy bedspread that would go with it.

"Let's go look at bedspreads," she said.

We started at a major department store. The minute we walked in, we saw it. The perfect fancy bedspread to go with my fancy gold velvet chair. It had black, brown, and gold stripes on one side, and black, brown, and gold swirls on the other. And it was on sale. Half-price.

It was called a "bed in a bag." The plastic bag contained a comforter, a top sheet, a fitted sheet, a dust ruffle, two pillow cases, and two pillow shams. As we looked at it more carefully, our elation de-elated. It was for a double bed. My bed was a queen.

We looked around for a queen-size "bed in a bag," but this was the only one on the shelf. We took it to the service counter and asked the lady if she could call other stores in the area to see if they might have it. She did. They didn't. Then we asked her to call some of their stores back in Indiana. She did. They didn't.

This particular "bed in a bag" had been discontinued. It was the only one in existence.

Now what? Buy it, or don't buy it? The pillow cases and shams would fit. The comforter, which was what I really wanted, would be fine—it just wouldn't come down on the sides of the bed as far as a queen-size comforter would. The bigger problem was, I was flying. The "bed in a bag" was huge. And heavy. If I bought it, I'd have to lug it with me back on the plane. I could just see me trying to shove this thirty-pound "bed in a bag" into an overhead compartment. I could check it as luggage and pay the extra price, but if I did that, the half-price comforter would then become full-price.

And, remember, it's still not going to fit the bed.

Diane knew I wanted to finish decorating my bedroom so I could get back to my writing, so she encouraged me to buy the "bed in a bag" and said she'd mail it to me.

When the box arrived, I put the dust ruffle on the bed (as best I could), the comforter on top of the bed, and the pillow cases and shams on my pillows. Not only did the bed look great, but now the bed matched the fancy, gold velvet chair.

Now, the second floor of my house is just one room with a pointed ceiling and windows at either end. At the top of the stairs, there's an alcove where I store some of my clothes. To hide the clothes, I had an old, faded, cotton quilt on a curtain rod. It had always looked okay—prior to getting the new chair and the new bedspread. Now, every time I went up and down the stairs, I could see how awful it really was. I decided to take the two sheets (that weren't going to fit the bed anyway) and make curtains, so the whole room would match.

But first, I had to take my sewing machine that didn't work across town to have it repaired.

Sixty dollars later, the sewing machine worked again. I made the curtains, ironed the curtains, hung the curtains, wasn't careful when I hemmed the curtains, and ended up with the bottoms being uneven. Decided I could get used to them. Couldn't get used to them. Tore the hem out of the curtains and re-hemmed them. Re-ironed them. Re-hung them.

Whew. I was done. Now I could sit in my chair and write.

No, I couldn't. There was no light. I needed some sort of light. A lamp. Actually, I needed three lamps—one for beside the chair and two for either side of the bed. It was time to replace the huge rooster lamp my mother once gave me (that I never liked) and the lamp made of seashells my mother once gave to my sister-in-law (who never liked it) who then gave it to me (who also never liked it).

Bought three matching lamps.

When I got them home, I realized I couldn't put them on my old night stands. Actually, I never did have night stands. On one side of the bed, there was an old table with rickety legs I'd bought in a garage sale. On the other side was a small wicker chest with rusted hinges that I'd had from childhood. Both were as pathetic as the old lamps.

I needed something fancy to go with the chair, the lamps, and the bedspread, so I set out to buy some night stands. Refusing to pay the prices they were asking at the furniture stores, and not finding anything fancy enough at Goodwill, I ended up with two modest black tables at the super discount store. $12.95. Now, here's where Sam entered the picture. The tables were too heavy for me to carry, so he came with me and carried them out to the car. And into my house. Where I asked him to assemble them. Did I mention they had to be assembled?

He started putting the first one together using my one (1) screwdriver despite his insistence that it wasn't the right size. How could it not be the right size? It was a screwdriver. As I sat on the couch with my feet up reading a book, I snuck glances at him out of the corner of my eye. Every so often he'd take his glasses off and rub his hand across his face, like he was trying to get rid of a bad headache. I'm used to him doing that. I think it keeps him from saying something he shouldn't.

Finally, he packed the tables up and said he'd finish assembling them at his house where he had his own tools (and, incidentally, his own large-screen TV with the ESPN channel). It took him about a day and a half, but he never complained. He probably figured that once my room was finished, he wouldn't have to go shopping with me anymore. Basketball season was beginning to overlap with football, and he was trying to keep up with both.

So, there I was with my new chair, my new bedspread, my three new lamps, and my two new tables. Then I thought, since I'm redoing the room, why don't I buy a new mattress? I couldn't remember the last time I'd bought a new mattress. Hey. If I got a better night's sleep, it might improve my writing.

I went to the super discount mattress store and bought a mattress. Figuring Sam might balk at the idea of carrying a queen-sized mattress on his back up the stairs, I had it delivered.

Still, it seemed like something was missing. Somehow the fancy gold velvet chair needed to be connected to the fancy bedspread with the brown and black swirls. A rug. It needed some kind of a rug. I spent the next week looking on line for area rugs. I spent hours looking at the discount stores and the stores in the mall. Then I walked into the Carpet Store and saw it. An elegant silk shag rug. It would be the perfect way to finish off the room.

The only rug they had was in forest green, which wouldn't work. So I ordered it in black and brown.

Word came back a week later—the manufacturer had discontinued that color. I returned to the store (across town) and looked at the color swatches. I selected my second choice: brown and beige. Word came back that that color had been discontinued as well. I went back to the store (across town) and selected color #3: gold with red flicks.

When the rug came in, Sam picked it up for me, hauled it

upstairs, and unrolled it. It was awful. The gold in the rug didn't match the gold in the chair. I hadn't noticed it before, but the gold in the chair was green. Very, very green. How can gold be green? Besides being the wrong color, it was also so shiny that it made the chair and the bedspread look dull. Plus, it was slippery. Every time I walked across it, I was going to have to have my cell phone with me to call 911.

I called Sam. He came over, rolled the rug up, put it in his car, and we drove across town and returned the rug.

"Let's stop at the mall," I suggested. A major department store was having a sale. In their home furnishings department I found a small gold and brown area rug. Perfect color. Perfect texture. Not the right size. I needed a rug that was 5' by 7'. This rug was 3' by 5'. Hey. If I bought four of them, I could lay them side-by-side. They were so silky, no one would see the seams.

It would work.

"No, it won't," Sam said.

"Yes, it will," I replied. I bought them.

Sam loaded them into his car, carried them upstairs to my bedroom, and laid them out on the floor. They looked terrible. They weren't the right shade of gold. How could there be so many different shades of gold?

Sam suggested I keep the four rugs and return the three lamps. If there wasn't so much light in the room, the rugs would look okay. Ha ha.

At that point, I seriously considered returning the chair, taking the bedspread back to North Carolina, and starting over from scratch.

On principle, Sam refused to help me return the rugs because he'd told me in the store they wouldn't work. Stuffing them into the bag they came in, I loaded them into my car by myself, lugged them into the mall, and took them to the service desk.

"Is there anything wrong with them?" the lady asked. I couldn't bring myself to tell her the whole story.

Returning to my computer, I began searching for a non-gold rug. I found a website for beautifully made hand-braided rugs. Very distinguished. Beautifully crafted. I found one that was brown and black. It would be perfect. I ordered it.

It arrived. It *was* perfect. The room was finally done.

The next morning when the alarm went off, I got out of bed and stepped on the new rug. It took off, with me on it, and I slid across the hardwood floor from one end of the upstairs to the other. My cat watched, fascinated, as I flew by. That must have been why the rug company had encouraged me to purchase a mat to go underneath the rug.

Another trip to the super discount store. They didn't sell rug mats. That meant another trip to another store. Realize, of course, that with all this shopping and returning, I'd gotten no writing done.

The next morning I had another surprise. My new rug had bumps in it. It had been shipped rolled up, but according to the literature, it would flatten out in just a few days. There were two distinct bumps.

I got down on my knees to smooth out the bumps. I couldn't. They remained bumps. Big bumps. With no small amount of irritation, I lifted up the rug and found ... two cat toys. My cat had decided to store them under the rug so she wouldn't have to go downstairs to get them.

I removed the cat toys and bought a mat to keep the rug in place. That's when I noticed the cat hairs. White cat hairs really show up on a brown and black rug. I bought a vacuum.

Finally, the room was done. I could sit in my fancy gold velvet chair and write.

In fact, I must write. A lot.

To pay for everything I bought for my special writing corner.

How I'd Change the World

If Jay Leno were to come up to me on the street and ask me how I'd change the world, I'd tell him I was happy with the world just the way it is. Of course, if I gave it some thought, I probably could come up with a few things that could be tweaked.

For instance, dust. I'd eliminate dust. Or, if dust has a purpose, someone should explain it to me.

Second, I'd make it easier to get band-aids out of their wrappers. (Am I the only one who has trouble with this?)

Third, I'd slow basketball down so I could see who had the ball.

Fourth, instead of the optometrist asking me: "Is this better ... or is *that* better?" *he'd* tell *me*. Aren't I paying him to tell me?

Fifth, there'd be a mountain in Indiana.

Sixth, everything at Macy's would be 80% off. Every day.

Seventh, red underwear would yell: "No! No!" if you threw them into the washing machine with your whites.

Eighth, husbands, boyfriends, and significant others would immediately jump up and take the garbage out if you asked them, even if it meant missing the last two minutes of a football game when their team was on the one yard line about to score a touchdown to win the game.

Ninth, ants would be trained to not go inside a house.

Tenth, cats would change their own litter boxes.

Eleventh, words that start with the letters "ph" but have the "f" sound (like "phone," "pharmacy," and "Philadelphia") would *start* with the letter "F."

Twelfth, the Pennsylvania turnpike wouldn't have ninety degree turns as soon as you come out of the tunnels, especially when you haven't been paying attention to the road, and especially when, if you miss the turn, you'll drive straight off the mountain.

Thirteenth, I'd make algebra easier by doing away with "x's," "y's," equal signs, and graphs.

Fourteenth, the container of ice cream would speak up when your significant other (boyfriend, or spouse) went to get a large bowl of it before he went to bed. It would say: "Would Sally (replace the name with yours) want you to be eating this?"

Fifteenth, I'd like someone to invent a mirror that would do me justice.

Sixteenth, teeth would never need fillings.

Seventeenth, knees would have shock absorbers that could be replaced every 5,000 miles.

Eighteenth, when you made sugar cookies from scratch, the dough would come out of the cookie cutters like the recipe says it will, instead of your having to poke your finger into the cookie cutter to get it out ... or pound the heck out of it on the counter.

Nineteenth, hair stylists would be able to lengthen your hair rather than just make it shorter.

And twentieth, when you're wearing a hat, and you take it off, your hair would look as good as it did before you put the hat on. No. Wait! Better. It would look better than before you put the hat on.

I'd be sure to point out to Jay Leno that these are not selfish changes. They wouldn't be just for my sake. They'd make life easier for a lot of people.

Plus, the world would be more beautiful.

Especially if there was a mountain in Indiana.

I'd really love to see a mountain in Indiana.

LOL WITH LOTS OF FRIENDS

An Afternoon with My Bridge Club

When I was growing up, everyone in my family played bridge. Except me. My parents were so "into" bridge, the night of my senior prom, after they helped decorate the gym for our after-prom party, they returned to our house, set up card tables in the living room, and played bridge with their friends until five in the morning, long after I had come home and gone to bed at three.

I could never understand why anyone would play bridge. It couldn't be fun. Everyone looked so serious. They didn't laugh or talk. How can you have fun if you don't laugh or talk?

Eventually, I did learn to play bridge, but it was because of a guy, not because of my parents. After he and I had dated for a couple of months, I realized we had practically nothing in common. I didn't want the relationship to end (he had tenure), so I decided to find something he liked to do that I could learn to do, too. He loved bridge, so that seemed the most obvious thing.

Our local YMCA offered lessons, so I went to sign up. I managed to step aside just as a hallway full of kids in their swim suits raced off to their learn-to-swim lesson. They seemed a lot more excited about learning to swim than I was about learning to play bridge.

Class met on Monday nights for eight weeks. Every week I showed up, and every week I hated it even more. To begin with, I'd never played cards before. I had to think twice to remember that a 10 was higher than a 9, that a 9 was higher than an 8, and so on down the line. Jacks, queens, kings, and aces were totally foreign concepts.

Second, I had to learn an entirely new vocabulary—one that made no sense. For instance, if you had a "book" it meant you had six tricks. Why would six tricks be called a "book"? When you laid your cards face up on the table, both the cards, and you, were called "the dummy." Who decided that? I even had to learn the four suits ... and what "no trump" was. OMG—"no trump" is really wicked to learn.

Basically, there were about 100 things I had to memorize before I could even start to play.

After each lesson, I'd be so discouraged, I'd sit in my car and cry. Then I'd give myself a pep talk. If I wanted to stay mentally alert and healthy (which I did), I needed to learn new things. So, every Monday night, I returned to the "Y" and tried not to get run over by the wet little kids returning from their swimming lessons.

Fifteen years later, the guy I was dating is long gone, but I'm still playing bridge with the ladies from that original class. But we play bridge our way. We tell jokes, show each other pictures of our kids and grandkids, compare our various aches and pains, share recipes, exchange books, and give reviews of any movies we've recently seen. Sometimes we talk during the round of play, not just in the breaks. No real bridge player would ever do that.

I finally figured out why bridge players are so crazy about bridge. It's mentally engaging. It keeps you on your toes. You have to concentrate and solve problems. And every now and then you can be devious and underhanded which, for me, fulfills an urge there aren't a lot of other socially acceptable ways I can express.

Yesterday, when we sat down to play bridge, Vera gave us the news that a friend of ours had just been diagnosed with Alzheimer's. We all expressed our concern about her, and our concern about someday getting it ourselves. To cheer us up, Vera said:

"But playing bridge is going to help. We're keeping our minds active."

She was right. It would be a long time before we started forgetting things because we *were* keeping our brains active. To show us doing that, I'd like to share with you a transcript of that afternoon's bridge game.

But first, in case you don't play bridge, here are some things you need to know:

1. In bridge, you play with two decks of cards. While the dealer is dealing one set of cards, her partner shuffles the second deck so the cards will be ready for the next hand. After the person who is shuffling shuffles (it's called "making the deck"), she puts the deck of cards on the table, to her right. Was that confusing? That might have been confusing. If you didn't get it, don't worry. Move on to item #2.

2. If you're the person who "won" the bid and are playing the hand, your partner is the dummy. She lays her cards face up on the table whereupon she can excuse herself to go to the bathroom or get something to eat or go play with Bev's cats which she locks in the bedroom, which I don't know why, because cats are very social and like to be with people. Also, if you've overestimated the value of your hand and have left your partner in the lurch, it's best to excuse yourself so you won't have to see her face when she realizes it.

3. The person playing the hand plays both sets of cards—the ones in her hand, and her partner's, which are on the table. It's important

that you remember if you're in your hand or "on the board" because there's no talking in bridge.

4. I forgot to tell you that. There's no talking in bridge. The only time you're supposed to talk is when you're bidding.

5. And finally, there's no showing emotion in bridge. It's like poker. No matter what disaster happens, you keep a straight face.

That said, here's a transcript of our game last Monday.

Me: "Whose turn it is to deal?"

Bill: "It must be Vera's."

Vera: "No. I dealt last time."

Bev: "Where are the cards?"

Bill: "I set them over there."

Me: "Why are they there?"

Bill: "Oh. I made them for Vera." (Vera has arthritis so sometimes we shuffle the cards for her.)

Me: "Then they should be over here."

Bev: "Well, if they're here, then it's your turn to deal."

I deal the cards. Everyone picks up their cards and arranges them into the different suits. As I'm arranging my cards, I notice that I only have twelve. I should have thirteen. I must have dealt someone an extra card and short-changed myself.

"I only have twelve cards," I announce. Bev and Bill count their cards. They each have thirteen. Obviously, I'd dealt Vera an extra card. So, Vera spreads her cards out, face down, and invites me to select one. I take that card, put it in my hand, and the game begins.

Long pause. They all look at me. They're waiting for me to bid.

Me: "Who dealt?"

Bill: "You did."

Me: "I did? Oh. Okay. Pass."

Bev: "Pass."

Bill: "One diamond."

Vera: "One heart."

Me: "One no trump."

Bev: "Pass."

Bill: "Two diamonds."

Vera: "Two hearts."

Me: "Two spades."

Bev: "Pass."

Bill: "Three spades."

Vera: "Pass."

Me: "Three spades? Three spades? Hmmm. I'm not sure what to do with three spades. Could we review the bidding?"

Vera: "I bid one heart."

Bev: "Wait. Bill opened."

Me: "No, he didn't. I opened."

Bev: "That's what I just said."

Eventually, we agree that I'm the person who's going to play the hand, and that I'm going to be playing three spades. The game begins.

I take the first trick. I then reach across the table to play a card from the dummy.

Bill: "Wait. You're in your hand."

Me: "I am?"

Bev: "You took the trick with the Ace in your hand."

Vera: "She took it on the board."

Bev: "No, she took it in her hand."

We finally agree that I took the trick with the Ace in my hand. (This dialogue—of trying to remember whether we took the trick in our hand or on the board—is repeated throughout the afternoon.)

I'm about to make a critical decision about which card to play next. The whole game will be determined by the card I play. Bill uses my pause to tell a joke:

"Did you know that my Aunt has teeth like the stars?"

The three of us wait for the punch line.

"They come out at night."

I laughed, but it blew what little concentration I had.

Then I suddenly noticed. I had five cards left in my hand. Bill and Bev each had three. Vera had only two. That meant the cards weren't dealt correctly and that my team was going to have to scratch the whole game. And we were winning!

I turned to Vera in a friendly manner and yelled: "Why did you give me one of your cards if you only had thirteen!"

Vera responded to me in the same manner: "Why did you ask me for a card if you had thirteen?"

We threw the cards in and began a new round.

Bev: "Whose deal is it?"

Bill: "It must be yours."

Bev: "Didn't I deal last time?"

Bill: "No, Sally dealt."

Vera: "Where are the cards?"

And that's how the afternoon went.

The important thing is, when we get together and play bridge, we have fun. And we're keeping our minds active. It will be a long time before we need to worry about forgetting things.

Wait. Whose turn is it to deal?

My Will

To: Linda@college.edu
Subject: My Will

Dear Linda:

I just came back from my attorney's office where I made out my will. You are now both the executor of my estate and my health care representative. I know we've talked about this on several occasions, but there are still a few things I think we should discuss. For instance, the opening line of my will says that I'm "of sound mind and memory." I didn't want to mention this to my attorney, but my memory is awful. Are they going to make me take a memory test in order for my will to be valid?

Also, it says in my "appointment of health care representative" document that you will "try to discuss with me the specifics of any proposed decision regarding my medical care and treatment if I am unable to communicate in any manner." I can see all sorts of problems with this. Worst case scenario: I am in a hospital bed talking to you clearly and you're sitting there saying to others: "Nope, I don't understand her."

Or, I can see you making an absurd decision saying "I'm sure that's what Sally would want" while I'm jumping up and down waving my arms yelling "No! No! That's not what I want!" The thing is: you're a dean at a major university, and you outrank me. The doctors and nurses are going to listen to you before they listen to me.

Having concerns,

Sally

To: SaraJane@college.edu
Subject: re: My Will

Hi Sally,

Got your email. Rest assured that you are of sound mind and, hopefully, memory. Although you've indicated to me that you occasionally have issues with memory, I will not hold that against you as your executor (executrix as a female executor, not executioner)—or as your health care representative, because I, too, have memory lapses—like remembering when I said "yes" to being your health care representative.

I will try not to let anyone know my status as a dean unless it will help you get what you want—not what I want—unless it's something we both want. We should probably come up with some signals, gestures, or signs that would make things clear—because I'm not good at 20 questions. I usually have 40 questions on top of my allotted 20. Question: how am I going to be able to "discuss with you the specifics of any proposed decision regarding your medical care" if you are unable to communicate? Maybe we should develop a system of sign language.

Try this: Let's say the doctor comes into your hospital room and tells me there's a way to extend your life two more days, but the procedure will be painful. I look into your sad, puppy eyes and read your expression. It says "Yes! I want two more days—I don't care about the pain. I want to live so I can watch *House MD* tomorrow night on TV."

Now, as your health care representative, I know you don't like pain, but I also know how much you enjoy watching *House MD*. As a dean, I make a decision—*House* over pain. I think we'll be fine if we have a system using signs and practice them beforehand.

There, I made a decision.

Worry Not,

Your HCR (Health Care Representative)

To: Linda@college.edu

Subject: My Will

Dear Linda (aka HCR):

You are correct. I would rather watch an episode of *House MD*—in pain—rather than miss *House* and NOT be in pain.

But, here's where it gets tricky. It all depends on whether or not it's a rerun. There are some reruns that I'd love to see again, like the episode where the little boy is abducted by aliens. However, there are other episodes I don't want to see again, like when Foreman gets sick. We're going to have to sit down together and classify the *House* episodes into two piles: "Sally definitely wants to see again" and "Sally would rather have her pain medication."

Love,

Sally

To: SaraJane@college.edu

Subject: re: My Will

Dear Sally,

I will make sure to have a *TV guide* with descriptions of the upcoming shows with me so we can plan your health care around the TV schedule. Priorities have to be set and maintained!

Love,

The Dean

To: Linda@college.edu
Subject: My Will

Dear Dean Linda:

   Your solution sounds all right on the surface, but I know you, and I know that you don't always keep the *Sunday TV guide* that comes in your Friday newspaper. Sometimes you do, but sometimes you throw it out. What if it's a week when you've thrown it out?
Worried All Over Again,
Sally

To: SaraJane@college.edu
Subject: re: My Will

Dear Worried Again:

   This will be easy. Picture this: you're in a hospital bed—deathly ill. I am sitting with you with my iPhone nearby. I simply type in the *TV guide* schedule in my Google search and come up with the local guide. Whereupon I will ask you to determine your preference—pass on to see your Maker, suffer in pain, or watch a particular show. You can blink your eyes—once, twice, or three times if you are not vocal at the time. How would that be?
Here for you,
Linda

To: Linda@college.edu
Subject: My Will

Dear Linda:

Great, except for the fact they don't let people use iPhones in the hospital.

Let's forget that for a minute and talk about your being the executor of my will. When I was making it out, my attorney asked me if I had anything of value in my house that I'd like to mention. I could think of two things—my Steinway piano, and my dolls. So, he put those things in my will. He referred to the three dolls as my "doll collection." I'm concerned that you may spend weeks trying to find a "doll collection" when you're going through my house.
Sally

To: SaraJane@college.edu
Subject: re: My Will

Dear Sally:

Are you talking about those three beat-up dolls at the foot of your bed?
Linda

To: Linda@college.edu
Subject: My Will

Dear Linda:

Yes.
Sally

To: SaraJane@college.edu
Subject: re: My Will

Dear Sally:
    Okay.
Linda

To: Linda@college.edu
Subject: My Will

Dear Linda,
    Me again. I thought of something else. You know, Suki is getting up there in years and one of these days she's not going to be with me. When that happens, I'm going to want to get a new kitten to keep Little Simba company while I'm at work. Here's the thing: my cats usually live to be about 20 years old. Which means that at some point, *you* might be taking care of them. Maybe you should go with me to pick out the new kitten.
Love,
Sally

To: SaraJane@college.edu
Subject: re: My Will

Dear Sally:
    Well, it won't be me that raises the kitten. It will be Bruiser. Maybe Bruiser should go with you.
Linda

To: Linda@college.edu
Subject: My Will

Dear Linda:

   Bruiser? Your golden lab? What's he weigh? 130 pounds?
Really Worried Now,
Sally

To: SaraJane@college.edu
Subject: re: My Will

Dear Really Worried,

   Back to my idea about using signals. We can teach the kitten to meow once if she's scared of Bruiser, twice if she's really scared, and three times if she feels her life is in immediate danger.
Hugs,
Linda

To: Linda@college.edu
Subject: My Will
Dear Linda,

   You've never had a cat, have you?
Sally

To: SaraJane@college.edu
Subject: re: My Will

Dear Sally,

Maybe you should just leave me the piano and the dolls.
Linda

Several Months Later

To: Linda@college.edu
Subject: My Will
Subject: Sad, sad news

Dear Linda:

I watched the last ever episode of *House MD* last night. They're ending the show. It's not going to be on next year. Write back. I need you. What's going to be left in life for me without *House*?
Sigh,
Sally

To: SaraJane@college.edu
Subject: re: My Will

Dear Sally,

Maybe you should start watching the weather channel. Or, I know. How about switching over and watching *Survivor*? Hey! If you get involved in *Survivor*, you might be motivated to stick around longer so you can see who the last person is to get voted off the island!
There for you,
Linda

My Most Memorable Book Signing

I would have had my driver's license if I hadn't been wearing my favorite pants. They weren't my all-time favorite pants. But they're my favorite pants to travel in because they have lots of pockets.

I was headed to Winston-Salem to do a book signing and had put my ticket and my driver's license in one of the pockets. But when I said good-bye to Sam (who'd driven me to the airport), my license must have fallen out onto the floor of the car. Because I didn't have it when the security guy asked me for it.

As I showed him my ticket—which I did have—I explained what had happened to my driver's license. I assured him he didn't need to worry. I knew exactly where it was.

He didn't care where it was. Without a government-issued ID— with a photo—he was not going to let me past security.

"Really?" I said, smiling at him.

"Really," he said, scowling back.

I thought for a second. What else could I use to identify myself? Aha! I had my university ID. It had my picture. Admittedly, I was having a *good* hair day when the picture was taken, and admittedly, today I was having a *bad* hair day. I showed him my card and explained that when I travel, I usually always have bad hair days. Regardless of the status of my hair, he rejected my university card as a valid form of identification.

I started going through my purse, pulling out different cards and putting them on his stand.

"Here's my Macy's card."

He rolled his eyes and repeated: "It has to be a government ID with a picture."

"Here's a coupon for a sale at Macy's. See, it has my name on it. No? Oh! Here's my bank card! I've banked at this bank for thirty years."

"It has to be a government-issued ID with your picture on it."

I pulled out my VISA card. My debit card. My insurance card. My AAA membership card. My library card. My check book. He kept shaking his head "no." Then I realized. I had it in my hand the whole time! My book! There was a picture of me on the back cover of my book.

"Look! This is me! I wrote this book. I'm on my way to Winston-Salem to do a book signing there. It's tonight!"

I could feel everybody in line behind me pulling for me. I mean, what kind of terrorist would draw that much attention to themselves?

He took a deep breath and the scowl on his face relaxed ever so slightly. I scooped everything back into my purse and raced to the scanner before he changed his mind.

Where I immediately set off the alarm because my favorite pants to travel in—the ones with all the pockets—have rivets and always set off the alarm. This was good. I repeat: what kind of terrorist would draw this much attention to themselves? The lady patted me down. I didn't mind. Maybe she'd find my driver's license.

My troubles continued when I got on the plane.

I was squashed into a window seat with a large body builder in the middle seat next to me. His tattooed arms and shoulders took up most of our entire row. He had several gold chains around his neck, and his head was shaved.

Now, wherever I go, I carry a pen and paper with me so I can jot things down. And I had some things I was itching to jot down. Like, telling people to be sure to have their driver's license with them when they travel. As best I could in the tight space, I dug through my purse for my pen. Which immediately fell to the floor. Not at my feet, which would have been bad enough. But all the way under my seat.

I had to have my pen. I wasn't going to be able to sit through the flight without writing down the things in my head. The ideas were already starting to back up. I considered asking the tattooed body builder to get it, but that would have meant he'd have to reach between my legs. Not such a good idea. So I said:

"I'm going to put my head in your lap to get my pen."

Which I proceeded to do. Neither one of us acknowledged that what had happened was anything out of the ordinary, which was fine with me, and probably even more fine with him.

My misadventures continued when I landed. My friend Diane and her daughter, Amy, picked me up at the airport. As soon as I stepped outside, I realized I'd brought the wrong clothes. It was cold. A lot colder than I thought it would be. I was going to freeze at the book signing if I didn't get something else to wear.

The book signing was going to be in just a few hours.

"We need to go to Macy's!" I cried. Diane and Amy rose to the call. Diane pealed out of the parking garage and pointed the car towards Macy's. Now, this was the first Saturday in December. Everyone in Winston-Salem was headed out to do their Christmas shopping. The people who weren't on the road were in Macy's. When we got to the store, Diane looked at her watch.

"We have about forty-five minutes."

"Then we need to separate!" I cried. "Amy—start here at the petites, take a dogleg to the left, and come up through the sweater dresses. Diane—start with the suits and circle around to the two-piece dresses. I'll do the sales racks and then head to Liz Claiborne. We'll meet in the dressing room in fifteen minutes."

In the dressing room, clothes flew. Amy took the clothes off the hangars and handed them to her mom. Diane pulled the outfits over my head while I stepped out of the previous ones. Success! We found the perfect "author's" outfit. A red and black sweater dress with a matching scarf that, from time to time, I could dramatically fling over my shoulder.

I bought the dress, we fought our way back through the crowds at Macy's, and we drove to Diane's. She reminded us we were tight on time.

Problem. The cute little red and black sweater dress, which looked adorable thirty minutes earlier in the store was so short, it barely covered my rear. Had none of us checked my rear in the store? Or, had Macy's mirrors been tilted so I would look taller and thinner? (I've always suspected their mirrors were tilted so I'd look taller and thinner.) Diane rummaged through her closet and brought me a pair of black boots and a pair of black tights. I tried them on. The shiny, black leather boots made it look like I was working in a nightclub instead of being an author at a book signing.

"What if you wore a pair of my black slacks?" Diane brought me a pair of her black slacks. She's a lot thinner than I am. I couldn't get them zipped.

She rummaged through her closet some more and found a pair of slacks with an elastic waist.

"Try these."

I got them on, but the elastic cut the top half of my body off from the bottom. Well, for two hours, I could suck it in.

We hopped in the car and, for the third time that day, fought our way through the Christmas traffic. But this time traffic was good. Hopefully everyone was going to the big bookstore to buy my book.

We arrived at 5:00 p.m.—right on time. The first thing I noticed was that the bookstore wasn't connected to a mall ... or to any other stores. It was back off the road all by itself. And there were only a few cars in the parking lot. But Eleanor—the lady I'd set up the book signing with—had assured me on the phone that 5:00 p.m. would be a great time for a book signing. We entered the store and asked for Eleanor. She arrived a few minutes later.

"Hello, Ms. Coffman! So nice to meet you," she said. She seemed a bit rattled. "I must tell you there's been a bit of a problem." She paused. "Your books didn't come in."

Huh?

"I don't know what the problem was. Something with the order. Perchance, do you have any copies of your book in the trunk of your car?"

Perchance I did. But my car was back in Indiana.

Eleanor excused herself, promising to return. Did we hear her correctly? There were no books? How were we going to have a book signing with no books?

Amy got on her iPhone and found that my book could be ordered online. So when people came in to buy my book, we'd have to send them to the service desk and have them order the book online.

Eleanor re-appeared a few minutes later and announced that our table was ready—complete with a sign. Follow her. We walked past the service counter, past the bakery and coffee area, past the history, government, self-help, autobiographies, and reference books, past the audio books, past the music section, and ended up in the children's section in the far corner of the store. The children's section? Would people looking for a humor book on being single find us in the children's section? Did anybody ever come back that far in the store—for anything?

And the "table." Did she say "table"? She meant "stand." It was just large enough to hold the bottle of water I'd brought. Diane, Amy, and I took our coats off and stood by this tiny little water-bottle sized stand. (To Eleanor's credit, there was a large, official poster with my name on it and a picture of the cover of my book.)

We must have looked official because a customer came up to me and asked: "Do you have any books on gardening?"

"I don't work here," I apologized. "How about a humor book on being single?"

That was all the excitement we had the first half-hour. Diane and Amy and I mostly just stood at our little table.

We stood.

And stood.

And stood.

It occurred to us that the only way we were going to sell a book was if our table was up near the front door. I tracked Eleanor down and asked if we could move.

"Oh, no," she said. "We never put authors near the front door. Especially at Christmas time."

And especially when you forgot to order my books.

I returned to the miniscule table in the back of the store. Diane and Amy were playing with some animal hand puppets that were on display.

"Hello, Mrs. Penguin. How are you?"

"I'm just fine, Miss Octopus, except we don't have any books to sell."

"It doesn't matter," said Baby Elephant. "Because we're here in the children's department and no one is going to see us anyway."

We played with the puppets for a while, then pulled up some

chairs and sat down. Since this was the children's department, they were children's chairs. Our knees came up to our chins.

Then, she appeared! A shopper with packages! Headed directly at us! Our first sale! We jumped to our feet.

"Could I ask you a question?" she said.

"Of course!" I said, ready to toss my (now very itchy) scarf dramatically over my shoulder.

"Could I leave my stuff with you while I use the ladies room?"

Oh, sure.

After she left, we went back to playing with the toys. There was a book that made the sounds of animals snoring. And a book that played "row, row, row your boat" whenever you turned the pages. There was a musical bubbles octopus we thought about playing with, but you had to fill it with water, and I was afraid Eleanor would catch us and make us buy the book.

A while later, another customer appeared, looking around like she was lost. This time, instead of waiting for her to approach me, I decided to make the first move.

"Are you looking for a book? I wrote a book. Here's a flier about my book. Do you like books?" I asked hopefully.

She looked uncomfortable. "You're really putting me on the spot here. Actually, I was just on my way to the ladies room." I moved aside and let her pass. She didn't even want us to watch her packages for her.

At 7:00 p.m. we put the hand puppets back on their stand, rolled the giant sign up, and headed to the car. We'd sold all of two books (to two of Diane's friends who—bless their hearts—were going to have to return to the store at some future date to pick them up).

I wasn't particularly upset or disappointed. I'd had a great time with Diane and Amy, and I had a new outfit from Macy's that had an itchy wool scarf that someday I'd be able to dramatically throw over my shoulder.

I only had one concern.

How I was going to fly back to Indiana without my driver's license.

How to Enjoy Being Single

Some people are single by choice. Others are single due to circumstances beyond their control. And then there are people, like me, who fall into a third category. We meet guys who live by the lyrics in the song "Marry Me." They'd marry me if they could just get up the nerve to say 'hello.'

There are a lot of neat things about being single. If I had the chance to give a newly-single person some advice on how to enjoy this lifestyle, here's what it would be:

The key to being single is to have lots of friends. You need different friends to do different things with. For instance,

Pat is my oldest friend. When we get together we talk about the things we used to do when we were young and stupid.

M.J. is my hippie friend who used to live in a commune. Being around her has taught me to be a lot less uptight about things.

I go shopping with Sam because he can find parking spaces, even during the holiday season. Plus, he can spot 80% off signs, and he carries my packages.

Lyn and I talk about spiritual things—angels, spirit guides, and soul groups.

Bev, Vera, and Bill are my bridge ladies. (We call Bill a bridge lady even though he's a guy). They tolerate me when I win (and get a swelled head), and don't make me feel bad when I lose.

Diane gives me unconditional love. She took me in one time after a traumatic breakup with a guy I'd been living with in another state. She didn't know she was going to take me in—I just showed up on her back doorstep with my two cats, one under each arm. She immediately took over. She found a place for the cats' litter box, put a blanket on a window sill so the cats could look outside at the birds, and then asked me what I wanted for dinner. (Years later, she admitted the cats had had fleas and she'd had to call an exterminator after we left.)

Linda is my most practical friend. She knows how to do anything. She's the first person I'd call if I accidentally ran over an ex-boyfriend with my car and needed help moving the body.

Rosie makes me laugh. When I have lunch with her, my food goes flying across the room.

Tom is my most creative friend. I call him when I want unusual, off-the-wall ideas.

Deb is my best friend at work. When one of us gets stressed, we put on oldies music and do the "stroll" down the hallway together.

Mary Kay can cook. I never turn down an invitation from her.

Karyn helps me figure out my relationship with my parents. Recently, she told me my folks thought I was "disorganized" the last time they came to visit. Of course I was disorganized! They came a day early.

Akesha has moved away, but I'll always remember the time she did my laundry for me. I'd been laid up with bronchitis for two weeks, and my apartment looked like a war zone with bronchitis-infected clothes lying all over. Akesha came over, picked up the clothes, and returned them the next day—soft, folded, and smelling like peaches. That was one of the sweetest things anyone has ever done for me.

What I'm saying is, you need all sorts of friends. You need at least one friend who'll tell you the dress you think you look great in is too tight. And at least one friend who won't.

As an introvert, I was never very good at making friends. The book that helped me learn was Dale Carnegie's *How to Win Friends and*

Influence People. I'm still an introvert, but he gave me some really good ideas on how to initiate conversations with people I don't know.

While you're getting Carnegie's book, check out Eckhart Tolle's *The Power of NOW.* He talks about finding joy in your life by living in the "present" instead of reliving the past or worrying about the future.

Now, as far as friends are concerned, be sure you hang out with people who are positive, upbeat, and fun, and avoid people who steal your energy or bring you down. (It's all right to do this. You're allowed to do this.)

Okay, now for the physical stuff. It's a lot more fun being single if you're in good health, so you need to find people who will help you make health-related decisions. When you're choosing a doctor, choose someone you can relate to. My mother always told me not to short-change yourself when it comes to doctors. Get the best.

Also, have ways other than your doctor to take care of yourself. I have an acupuncturist, an herbalist, a massage therapist, a chiropractor, a physical therapist, and a personal trainer who I see at different times for different things. I also have a group of people I do yoga with and another group I meditate with.

If you don't have someone in your life to spoil you, then you need to spoil yourself. Get a foot massage from the Asian lady at the mall who has that booth you always walk past. Or, the next time you're at the airport, get a neck massage from the guy who has that weird-looking massage chair.

Now for your head. I think people should daydream on a regular basis. I do this all the time. Let's say I'm in a really boring meeting at work. What I'll do is start singing "Now, I've ... had ... the time of my life" in my head and pretend I'm dancing with Patrick Swayze. When the meeting gets really boring, I run across the room and jump into his outstretched arms and he lifts me up over his head. (Be careful, though. If you're going to do this, you don't want to look too happy. If you look too happy at a staff meeting, your boss is going to call on you and ask you for your opinion about something of which you won't have one because you haven't been paying attention.)

Also, on the topic of your head, take good care of your emotional side. I think it's important to acknowledge and experience all sorts of different emotions. Want passion? Go to an opera. Want your heart rate to go up? Go to a scary movie ... or ride on a roller coaster. Feel like screaming? Go to a basketball game. Looking for awe and wonder? Step inside a place of worship. Want to laugh? Check your TV guide. My favorite programs used to be *MASH* and *Northern Exposure*, but now I watch *The New Adventures of Old Christine*. I love Julia Louis-Dreyfus's character—she's almost as self-centered as I am.

If you want to experience lots of emotions, grab a friend and take a trip. Or, go on your own. Visit a country where English isn't the primary language. Whitewater raft down the Colorado River—especially if you're a city girl. Walk across Scotland. Do something daring and exciting. Traveling gets you to meet people you wouldn't ordinarily meet, gives you intellectual stimulation (which will make you a more interesting person), and will teach you to "bend and stretch" (and that will keep you young).

Of course, when you travel, you have to be prepared to leave your comfort zone. I took a two-week trip overseas one time when I was addicted to caffeinated soft drinks. The whole time I was there, I couldn't find any. Not one. At the airport on my way home, I spotted a guy wearing a shirt with the Coke insignia on it. My hands around his neck, I banged his head against the wall and screamed: "I need a coke—now!" When he was finally able to speak, he explained that it was his dad's shirt. He'd just borrowed it for the trip.

Okay. Some final thoughts. Don't sit around waiting for people to call you. They're too busy. I used to keep track about whether it was my turn to call someone or their turn to call me. Then I realized—it doesn't matter. I call them.

Handle your money wisely. It's a lot more fun being single with money than without. And finally,

Try not to think of your problems and mistakes as problems and mistakes. Try to think of them as adventures. For example, the toilet in the hotel I was staying in the other night backed up at 6:00 a.m. I called the front desk. They said they'd send someone up with a plunger. Was I upset? Heavens, no. The only thing I wondered about was: what's the appropriate attire for hosting a guy with a plunger in your hotel room at 6:00 a.m.?

Well, I have to go now. One of my friends just called—she accidentally ran over her ex-boyfriend and needs my help hiding the body.

And that, my friends, are what good friends are for.

Hey—why don't you join us?

Bring a shovel.

MEN

Driving Miss Sally

I used to have a chauffeur. Not in this lifetime. In one of my other lifetimes. I have a vivid memory of standing in the back of a chariot telling the driver to slow down, speed up, and use his turn signals.

In this life, I ride in Sam's SUV and correct his driving from the passenger's seat.

It's not that Sam's a bad driver. It's just that he and I drive differently. For instance, when I drive, I like to leave a few inches between my car and the car in front of me. I use my turn signals. And I keep my hands on the steering wheel. Sam keeps his hands on the wheel, too, unless he's describing something he needs both hands for— like demonstrating the length of a pass Drew Brees threw in his last football game.

Then, there are our responses to traffic lights. When I'm driving and I see the light up ahead turn yellow, I begin to slow down. By the time I get to the red light, I've come to a smooth and gentle stop. When *Sam's* driving, he's so busy watching things along the side of the road that he doesn't see the yellow light until he's right up on it, whereupon he slams on his brakes. My head flies forward toward the front window, then backwards and hits the head rest. When the light turns green, he stomps on the accelerator to make up for the time he lost sitting at the red light.

Then there are curves. Sam is the only person I know who can drive around a ninety degree curve while looking in the opposite direction.

This brings us to road barriers and traffic signs. Sam sees nothing wrong with driving around a road barrier if it will get him where he wants to go. I, on the other hand, am totally sign-obedient. If a sign says: "Watch for ice on bridge," I do. Even in the summer. Or, let's say Bruce Willis (in one of his bad guy roles) is chasing me in his Batmobile (wrong movie?) and I come up to a one-way street, and that one-way street is the only way to get away. If there was a clearly visible sign saying "Do Not Enter"—even if there were no other cars in the road—I would not be able to go down that street the wrong way.

This brings us to staying in the lane you're driving in. Sam was driving straight down the white center line on an interstate highway the other day.

"What lane are you in?" I asked him.

"The left."

"Well, I'm in the right."

This brings us to navigation. Sam and I make critical navigational decisions differently. Take the time we were driving on I-65 from Lafayette to Louisville on a Friday afternoon in rush hour. Just south of Indianapolis, there was a yellow flashing light on an overhead sign alerting us of a crash up ahead. It read: "Expect Severe Delays."

Sam ignored the sign. We drove on. There was a second warning. Then a third.

Three flashing signs? All saying the same thing? I jumped into action. I opened the glove box, unfolded the map of Indiana, and started looking for alternative routes. How many ways were there to get to Louisville? I began analyzing them. Which way would be the shortest? The fastest? The one with the most McDonald's in case we got hungry or I had to go to the bathroom?

I told Sam to turn off at the next exit.

He responded by turning the radio up and continuing to drive in the long line of traffic going three miles an hour.

"What are you doing? We have to get off. We can't sit in this traffic all day." I reopened the map that I had so carefully folded up. I searched for another route.

"Get off at the next exit."

Sam drove on by.

Now, when Sam makes a decision—no matter how wrong it is— he doesn't change his mind. Twenty minutes later, after only moving about two miles, he begrudgingly got off on a side road. Of course, by then, everyone *else* had gotten off and we were stuck in the same traffic as before, confirming in his mind that we should have stayed on the main highway.

Let's divert from the subject of driving for a minute and I'll give you another example of how differently Sam and I solve problems. Picture us at the mall. Let's say, for instance, that we both need to buy a new pair of boots. (You need boots in Indiana because Indiana has about seven months of winter weather. Four months of winter and seven months of winter weather.)

Here's Sam. He'd go to the store closest to where he parked and buy the first pair of boots he saw. Actually that's not true. He wouldn't even be shopping for boots. In the winter, he wears a pair of beat-up old tennis shoes and then complains that his feet are always wet. Well, if he were to buy a pair of boots, it would be the first pair he saw.

I, on the other hand, shop using the comparison/contrast method. I look at every pair of boots in every store, then buy a pretzel at Mr. and Mrs. Pretzel and review my options. The black boots at Store #1 were a perfect fit, but they didn't come up quite as high on my leg as I wanted them to. The brown boots at Store #2 were within my budget and came up to the right spot on my leg, but they were suede. I wanted leather. The boots at Store #3 were neither comfortable, the right size, nor the right color, but the salesman flirted with me so I should at least go back and take another look in case, in the meantime, maybe a customer with bigger feet had tried them on and stretched them out. After considering the pros and cons of all the boots, I then go back to buy the first pair I looked at. And usually discover that someone just bought them, and I have to start over from scratch.

Okay. Back to my story. The one good thing about riding in the car with Sam is that we're both able to have our needs met.

My need is to correct people when they don't do things the way I think they should.

Sam's need is to not let my suggestions annoy him.

Which he does by simply leaning forward and turning up the volume on the radio.

Men in the Ladies' Restroom

Yesterday at the mall, I'd finished my shopping and was headed home. I needed to go to the bathroom, but decided I could wait. I'd rather use my own bathroom rather than a public one. Then my bladder sent a stronger, more urgent message. It needed to go—now. So I headed to the ladies' room outside of Sears.

I'd been shopping for several hours and was tired. I had two large shopping bags—one in each hand. I also had a thousand things on my mind, like, should I stop at the grocery on my way home? Was there anything that couldn't wait until tomorrow? Where was I going to put my shopping bags when I was in the stall? I shouldn't put them on the floor. But if I didn't put them there, where?

I'd been to this ladies' room before. There are no doors to push open—you enter through a maze. And when I entered, there they were.

Three men.

I stopped abruptly. What were three men doing in the women's restroom?

They were lined up on the far side of the room, facing the wall. I took a long, slow look. It looked like they were each holding something. What?

Then it hit me! Guns! They were holding guns! Should I yell for help? Should I run? If I ran, should I take my shopping bags with me?

Then it hit me! They were at urinals. Someone had put urinals in the women's restroom!

As I was processing this information, I saw another man, to my right. Then—to my left—another!

Then it hit me! I was in a unisex bathroom! If that was the case, though, where were the other women?

Then it hit me! I was in the men's room.

"I'm so sorry!" I cried, raising my shopping bags to cover my eyes.

The gentleman on my right said politely: "That's all right."

"I'm so sorry!" I cried again. I began backing out of the room. I hit the wall. I followed the wall with my back until I got out of the maze and into the ladies' room next door. And I stayed there a long time. I didn't want to run into any of those men again.

To be perfectly honest, I think someone switched the restrooms from the last time I was there.

In case they switch them again, I'm going to start reading the signs.

Dating After Forty

Dating is hard enough when you're young, but it gets infinitely more difficult as you get older. I'm not exactly sure when things change. For me, it was around age forty. At forty, you have an entirely new set of challenges.

For those of you approaching forty and thinking about dating, here are some of my observations and advice:

First: People you don't even know are going to want you to die a slow, painful death. These people are called ex-wives. Once they find out about you, they'll be hoping you fall through a manhole, get eaten by a shark, or burn in hot lava. In fact, they'll be more than willing to provide the manhole, the shark, and the volcano. Don't take it personally.

Second: Avoid dating people who aren't yet over their ex'es. I once had a date with a recently-divorced pediatrician. The first half of the evening was fantastic—we laughed, had dinner, and laughed some more. Then came the second half of the evening. The topic of Thanksgiving came up, and he began reminiscing about the Thanksgivings he'd had with his wife. The evening ended with him crying on my shoulder (literally) and me giving him suggestions on how to get her back.

Third: The people you go out with may have some flaws. The best you can hope for is that their flaws will be compatible with yours.

Here's my experience with this:

An outdoorsy kind of guy who worked in my building caught

my attention. He dressed differently from the other men who worked there. Instead of wearing chinos and polo shirts, he wore jeans and the kind of shirts Jeff Probst wears to host *Survivor*. Instead of carrying a briefcase, he carried a beat-up Army shoulder bag.

I knew he'd been in the military, had worked with explosives, and had some hearing loss. He'd mentioned that once when we were in the elevator together. And that was about all I knew about him. Wanting to get to know him better, I invited him to a seminar I was getting ready to attend. He said he'd like to go with me.

We entered the seminar room just as the first speaker was being introduced. There were two empty seats near the back of the room, so I slipped into one and he took the other.

As soon as I sat down, I remembered—he had problems with his hearing. And I'd chosen a seat in the back of the room!

Feeling terrible, I wrote "Can you hear from back here?" in my notebook and showed it to him. He reacted by patting his chest.

That was weird. I waited for an answer.

Instead of speaking, he patted the upper part of his right leg.

Then the upper part of his left leg.

Still no answer.

Oh-Kay.

I tried to appear nonchalant as he went back to patting his chest. But it was clear—I'd done it again. I'd managed to find another loser.

I toyed with the idea of getting up and leaving. I'd have to step over him to get to the door, but he was patting with such urgency I was sure he wouldn't notice.

Next, he bent over and groped around in his backpack. After that, he returned to patting the pockets of his shirt. I was half-way out of my seat when he found what he was looking for.

His glasses. He needed glasses to read the note that asked him if he could hear.

He wasn't a loser—he was just missing some of his senses.

This brings me to my fourth, and final, piece of advice: Be prepared to say (and do) things you never would have considered saying (or doing) when you were younger. For example:

A friend of mine once fixed me up with a pilot. He was tall, dark, and handsome. And he had tenure. He said he was going to take a new jet up for a test-flight that evening. Did I like flying? Would I like to come along?

Those two questions had two entirely different answers. Did I like flying? No. Especially in small planes. I vowed never to go up in a small plane again after a flight I took one time from Honolulu to Maui. It was a four-seater plane with a tiny cargo area. Our cargo was a Great Dane that slobbered on my shoulder and weighed so much we were barely able to take off. The fourteen-year-old pilot, who was practicing to be a stunt pilot, kept dive bombing towards the ocean whenever he spotted a whale. After circling the whale, he'd return as far up into the stratosphere as he could so he could dive bomb again.

I closed my eyes and held my stomach, trying to keep my Meitei and pineapple chicken salad down. My hands, which were tucked into my armpits, froze in that position. It took two men—one on each side—to lift me off the plane when we landed, and it took about twenty-four hours before my muscles relaxed enough for me to get my hands out of my armpits.

But what I really dislike about flying are the take-offs and landings. The wings wiggle, the plane rocks from side to side, and there are weird noises. Flying level is somewhat bearable, but I hate take-offs and landings.

So, no, I did not want to go for a test ride.

On the other hand, he was tall, dark, and handsome. And he had tenure.

So, in answer to his question; "Would you like to come along?" I smiled my sexiest smile and said: "What time?" There weren't a lot of whales in Indiana, and surely I could handle a single take-off and landing.

Wearing my little black dress, I met him at the airport. I "oohed" and "awhed" (as I thought I should) over the plane. Then I followed him up the steps, selected a seat, and fastened my seat belt. While he completed checking things off on his check list, I practiced crossing my legs. I tried several different positions before I came up with the one I was happy with.

Then he turned around in his seat and said: "By the way. I'm going to be practicing take-offs and landings." And off we went.

Now, in telling these stories, in no way do I mean to discourage you from dating if you're over the age of forty. You'll be fine.

Just stay flexible ... and develop a sense of humor.

You'll definitely need a sense of humor.

Thank You Notes

𝒟ear Dirk, Brick, and Mick:

By the authority vested in me as your Aunt, I hereby suspend all future gifts of cash, gift cards, checks, presents, McDonald's coupons, and airline tickets until which time I receive—in your own handwriting—thank you notes for the Christmas presents I sent you two months ago.

Said thank you notes should include (but not necessarily be limited to) the following three things: a description of the present, a statement of how much you appreciated receiving it, and a sentence convincing me that you're using it— and enjoying it—even if you aren't.

This is the way things are done in a civilized world.

Long live civilization!

Signed,

Auntie Sally

Meeting Tom's Mother

This is the story of the time Tom took me home to meet his parents.

We weren't engaged, or living together, or anything like that. We were just dating. We had plans to spend Saturday with my brother and sister-in-law in Chesterton, and since Tom's parents lived in the next town over, it seemed logical to stop by their house and say "hello."

His dad, I wasn't worried about. His mother, though, had been a drill sergeant in the Marines. I'd seen a recent photo of her. She was a large, sturdy woman. She still looked like a drill sergeant.

His parents were waiting for us at the front door when we pulled in. Tom introduced us, we all shook hands, and then we went and sat down in the living room where there were doilies on the arms of the couch and all the chairs. Tom and his dad started talking about the Chicago Cubs. His mother asked if I'd like to go see her garden.

Oh. Sure.

The garden was out in the "back forty," so she pulled on the boots that were setting next to the back door, and off we went. We both waited for the other one to start the conversation. His mother was the first to speak.

In complete seriousness, and out of the clear blue sky, she asked: "Do you think you're going to grow any?"

Grow any what? I wondered. Taller? Was I going to grow any taller? I've been asked a lot of things in my life, but I have to admit, I didn't see that one coming. I was in my mid-thirties. The odds were slim that I was going to grow any taller. So the first answer that came to mind was: "No."

But maybe it was a trick question. I decided to think before I answered.

I could be apologetic: "I think I've grown as much as I can."

Or, I could be sarcastic and say: "I wouldn't count on it if I were you."

I knew she was probably trying to get at something. But what? I decided to keep thinking until I figured it out.

Think. Think. Think.

There *was* about a foot difference between my height and hers (and Tom's). Maybe she was hoping for grandchildren. If so, she probably wanted them to be tall so they could be Marines. That made sense. But still not wanting to jump to any conclusions, I continued walking, and thinking.

Then it hit me! Maybe she wasn't thinking about grandchildren at all. Maybe she was asking about our sex life. Maybe she was worried that since Tom was so much taller than me, that he might be hurting me. Yes. That was it. Wanting to reassure her, I said:

"Oh, he's very gentle."

To which, she had no response.

We stood there, side-by-side, looking at the cornstalks, zucchinis, and tomatoes, trying to process what the other had said. After a while, we turned and headed back to the house. Neither of us said anything more. By that time, Tom and his dad had finished predicting the future of the Cubs and were standing in the driveway. The four of us shook hands again, and Tom and I drove off.

I never told him about the conversation.

And I never grew any taller.

Years later, Tom ended up marrying someone taller than me, and I think his mother was very happy. But my answer: "He's very gentle" to her question: "Do you think you'll grow any?" had to be the most bizarre conversation two people have ever had.

Saying "Break a Leg" is not Enough

To: All the men in my Wilderness Survival class who came to my opening night.

First of all, let me say that the flowers you sent were beautiful. They were sitting on the counter in my dressing room when I arrived at the theatre. Sending an actress flowers for her opening night is a thoughtful, generous gesture as well as an old, established theatrical tradition.

There is another equally important tradition in the theatre—that is, going backstage after the show to congratulate the cast. Especially if you know someone in the cast. Actors want immediate feedback on how they did. Well, actually, they don't want feedback on how they did. They want to hear that they were wonderful and that the play could not have gone on without them. Phrases like: "You were great!" repeated over and over are appropriate, readily accepted (and believed), and will score points for the audience member/congratulator/person dating the actress.

However, when an actress does not see the audience member she invited to the play, she is going to want answers to the following questions.

Regarding the performance of *California Suite* that you attended:

1. Which of the four acts did you like the best? (Reminder: I was only in Act Four.)
2. In that act, which of the four characters did you like best? (There's only one right answer to this one, as well.)

3. Which of my lines did you like the best? Second best? Third best?
4. Which of my lines did you laugh hardest at?
5. As an audience member, did you make a conscious effort to get the people around you to laugh? Explain the various techniques you used.
6. After I was onstage for a while, did you turn to the people around you and say "Isn't she good?" If so, I didn't hear you. Do you have any witnesses who could confirm you made positive comments about my acting ability during the show?

Helpful Hints: Answers will be evaluated on creativity, length, degree of lavish praise, and extent of exaggeration. Completing this questionnaire will go a long way in increasing your chances of having a relationship with this actress in the future.

My Worst Blind Date

I've had some pretty bad blind dates in my life, but my all-time worst blind date was with my best friend Suzanna's older brother Dwayne.

Dwayne (who lived in Chicago) was going to be in town for a few days, and Suzanna got the bright idea to fix us up. In fact, she decided that she and her husband Richard could come on the date with us. It could be a double date! Hating both blind dates and double dates, I was set to decline the invitation until she mentioned that Dwayne was an attorney. Oh. It might be fun to date a suave, sophisticated lawyer from the Windy City. Plus, I was young and stupid. So I agreed to go.

By agreeing to go, I was violating the first rule of blind dating—drive to the location yourself, so you can leave when you want. I was also violating Rule #2: keep it short. Dinner is okay. Lunch is better. Coffee in a crowded coffee shop is best.

I wasn't worried in this case, though. Suzanna was my best friend.

Now, what should I wear? What did successful career women in Chicago wear? I decided on a cashmere sweater with dress slacks and heels. And what would we talk about? Was he going to think I was a hick?

Saturday night arrived. There was a knock on my front door—I was about to find out.

I opened the door. A short, chubby little guy with thick glasses greeted me with a cheerful "Hi!" He moved his arm in a wave from one side of his body to the other while grinning from ear to ear.

My brain tried to process what my eyes were seeing. This guy obviously had the wrong door. This couldn't be Dwayne.

"I'm Dwayne!"

Impossible! *This* was Suzanna's brother—the sophisticated attorney?

Behind his goofy glasses, Dwayne's eyes looked huge, like a fish. He wore a turtleneck, a plaid blazer that came nowhere near closing in the front, wrinkled khakis, and tennis shoes. And I'd been worried about what I was going to wear?

I checked again with my brain. Was there any way I could get out of this? Nothing came to mind. I was going to have to go through with it. I smiled weakly, got my purse, and reminded myself it was just dinner. I could make it through dinner.

As we approached Richard's car, I could see that he and Suzanna were as psyched about the evening as Dwayne was. Suzanna was honking the horn and leaning out the window waving. Richard stepped out and pulled his seat forward so Dwayne and I could squeeze into the back. As soon as I got in, the three of them gave me the exciting news:

"Guess where we're going for dinner?"

"To our favorite restaurant!"

"In Indianapolis!" they cried. And off we went.

Now, Indianapolis is an hour away. Figuring an hour to drive there, two hours for dinner, and another hour to drive back home, I was looking at a good four hours before I'd be back home. I started my mental clock. Four hours to go.

Suzanna, Richard, and Dwayne started swapping family stories and laughing uproariously. Anyone watching them would think they were drinking (they weren't). I had no idea who the characters in the stories were, or what the stories were about, so I listened and smiled weakly.

Amidst the hilarity, I suddenly found Dwayne's hand on my leg. I removed it and put it back in his lap.

A few minutes later, he put his hand on my leg again. I removed it. Again.

And again.

And again.

Then it hit me. Not only was I trapped in the cramped backseat of a car with Dwayne, but Dwayne was horny.

I kept hoping Suzanna would notice what her brother was doing there in the backseat, but she was oblivious.

The next thing Dwayne tried was putting his arm around my shoulder. I slapped it away. He tried again. I rammed the heel of my high heeled shoe into the top of his ratty tennis shoe. Suzanna continued telling jokes and stories while I continued slapping and kicking her brother in the backseat. If I made it through the evening, I was going to kill her.

Obviously on my own back there, I planned my last line of defense. I scooted as far away from Dwayne as possible, put my back up against the door, and pulled both legs up to my chest. Now, if need be, I could use *both* legs and get some real power into my kicks.

At least I was working up an appetite for the fancy dinner in the fancy restaurant they'd promised me. I was going to order the most expensive thing on the menu. A steak. Or a lobster. Or a steak and a lobster.

When we pulled into the restaurant's parking lot, I checked my watch. It had taken exactly one hour to get there. Three more hours to go.

As I extracted myself from the car, I looked up and saw the sign above their "fancy," favorite restaurant.

It was a fast food hamburger chain. Their favorite place to eat—the place they'd talked about with such excitement—was a fast food hamburger chain. I'd gotten all dressed up to eat at a fast food hamburger chain.

The only thing I remember about dinner was sitting in a booth with bright lights glaring down on us, which, I hoped, would keep the place from being robbed. The only thing on the menu was greasy hamburgers and French fries. Suzanna, Dwayne, and Richard enjoyed the meal thoroughly. I was simply thankful that dinner didn't take long.

As we got back to the car, I pulled Suzanna into the back seat with me. The ride home was much more subdued. We were each in our own little worlds trying to digest those slimy, greasy, little hamburgers.

I never saw Dwayne again, and Suzanna and I never discussed that evening.

But a year later, she attended Dwayne's wedding and reported that he and his bride served those greasy, fast food hamburgers at their reception.

My Dad

I think I was supposed to be born into my Uncle Jim's family, but at the last minute, plans changed, and I ended up in Fred and Dorothy Coffman's family.

I think what happened was, God knew I was going to need a dad for a long time. Uncle Jim died at an early age, so He moved me over to Uncle Jim's *brother's* family. By having Fred and Dorothy as my parents, I could still be part of the Coffman clan and still have Aunt Mary Jane and Grandma Coffman as members of my family.

My Uncle Jim would have made a great dad for me, but let me tell you about the dad I ended up with.

Maurice Fred Coffman was twenty-two when WWII broke out. He badly wanted to enlist, but couldn't pass his physical—his blood pressure was too high. The doctor told him to go walk around the building and come back. His blood pressure was still too high. He went back outside and walked some more. He walked all morning until (I can't remember which), either the doctor gave in, or his blood pressure was finally within the right range.

During the war, my dad got married and started a family. He was raised in a generation where a man's role in life was to be a provider. And he was. He and my mom got the three of us kids everything we needed. (We could have anything we "wanted" as long as we saved up our own money to buy it.)

He also took care of his family. To keep my mom safe, he regularly bought *her* new tires for our car. When it was cold outside and the family was going someplace, he'd go out to the garage, back the car out, and warm it up for us.

My dad felt strongly about education. He sent all three of us kids to college. It was *expected* that we'd attend college.

My dad had a quiet (but strong) conviction to his faith. He took us to church every Sunday—in fact, we were always the first ones there. I remember we'd sit in the car (in the wintertime), or stand at the door (in the summertime), and wait for the janitor to come and unlock the building. The minister finally gave my dad his own key. My dad served on committees, ushered, and stayed after the service to help count money. He also had the ability to quietly persuade people who moved into our neighborhood to join our church.

My dad enjoyed meeting people. As a marketing executive for a railroad, he was expected to "wine and dine" executives from other railroads and from companies that his railroad wanted to do business with. A quiet man (not an extrovert), he enjoyed a good conversation. When I'd listen to him discuss an issue with someone, it was often hard for me to tell which side he was on. He'd find out as much as he could from the other person and have a truly intellectual discussion.

My dad always had friends—golf buddies, church buddies, and bridge buddies. For as long as I can remember, he'd invite people over on the weekends to watch sports on our TV—one of the first in the neighborhood. Even into his later years, when he had to give up playing golf, going to church , and going out to play bridge because he could no longer drive, he still enjoyed watching sports with friends.

My dad was devoted to my mother for their sixty-five years of marriage. When my mother passed, he moved into a retirement home and got to know everyone there. Whenever he went down to the dining room (three times a day), he'd stop and ask people how their grandson's high school graduation went, how their visit from their nephew from Arizona went, how they were feeling, and what their plans were for the day. He always made a point to introduce himself to new residents and show them around. When there was a fire drill, he made sure Jeanne, who lived next door, made it out of her apartment all right.

My dad had great personal strength. One time I went with him to an appointment with his oncologist. (I didn't know he'd been seeing an oncologist.) Apparently he had a spot on one of his kidneys. The doctor had us both sit down, then looked him in the eye and said: "There's nothing more I can do for you. I'd advise you to go home and get your affairs in order." My dad shook his hand, thanked him, and we went back to the car. I immediately started crying.

"What are you crying about?" he said half-gruffly.

"Because of what the doctor just told you!"

To which he (matter-of-factly) said: "Oh, you take things too seriously."

That afternoon, he got a call from his heart doctor. I could hear the doctor say: "There's nothing more we can do for you. I'm sorry. You should probably get your affairs in order." Who would get that news twice in one day?

That was three and a half years ago. Needless to say, he didn't take their predictions seriously.

Sam and I flew to Philadelphia to help celebrate his ninety-second birthday. When we arrived, he asked us to take him to the dentist—he had "a bit of a toothache." After looking at the tooth, the dentist told him he needed a root canal. "Would you like me to do it right now?" she asked. He said "yes." So Sam and I waited in the waiting room while he had a two-hour root canal.

If it'd been me, I'd have wanted to go home and rest, but not my dad. We were his guests, and he insisted on taking us out to dinner. After dinner, I thought he'd want us to leave, but not my dad. He wanted to rehearse. The next day, he and Sam and I were going to put on a short "program" for the residents of his retirement home. We were going to read some jokes and funny stories. So, that night we sat in his room and rehearsed.

When my dad did something, he did it well. The next morning he wanted to rehearse again, so we did. Then we went down to the lobby where we were going to perform. Sam and I decided to stand on the stairway to read our pieces. There was room at the bottom of the staircase for Dad to perform sitting in his scooter.

Well, when it came time for the performance, he got out of his scooter and leaned on the handrail at the bottom of the stairs. I argued: "Dad, this is going to last for about fifteen minutes. You don't want to stand for fifteen minutes. Just stay in your scooter."

And he said: "I'm going to stand."

I tried several more times, and then I realized the man was going to stand.

And by golly, he stood.

He gave a great performance. After we finished the reading, someone came up to me and asked: "How long has your dad been performing?" The fact is he'd never done anything like that before.

Before Sam and I returned to Indiana, I asked Dad if he needed us to run to the store for him. No. He didn't need anything. The next evening, I called him:

"Hi, Dad! What did you do today?"

"Went to the grocery store."

"You told me yesterday that you didn't need anything!"

"I changed my mind."

"How did you get there?"

"The bus."

"You took the bus? With your scooter?"

"No, I used my walker."

"You did? Well, what did you get?"

"Just a watermelon."

"A watermelon?! How did you carry a watermelon?"

"It was just a small one."

He was ninety-two. He bought a watermelon. Using his walker. Taking the bus. And this was three and a half years after the doctors had told him to put his affairs in order.

There's a joke about a talking centipede that captures my dad's spirit.

A man decided he wanted to buy an unusual pet. So he bought a talking centipede. It came in a little white box.

He took the box home, found a good spot for it, and decided he would start off by taking his new pet to church. So he asked the centipede, "Would you like to go to church with me today?"

No answer.

This bothered him a bit, so he waited a few minutes and then asked again. "How about going to church with me?"

No answer.

So he waited a few more minutes.

He decided to try one last time.

He put his face up against the centipede's house and shouted: "Hey, in there! Would you like to go to church with me?"

This time, a little voice came out of the box.

"I heard you the first time. I'm putting my shoes on!"

I think my dad spent his entire life "putting his shoes on."

He passed shortly after his ninety-second birthday. I don't have him anymore, but I do have the things he taught me:

Whatever your mother says, goes.

When you see a roadside stand, stop and buy fresh corn.

Do your work first, and then you can go out and play.

Give little kids nickels. (He always carried change in his pockets.)

Dads can go a whole lifetime getting ties, handkerchiefs, and belts as presents.

Don't buy something until you have the money for it.

Apologize correctly the first time so you don't have to go back and do it again.

Check the air in your tires.

Change your oil.

Tell the truth ... and take the consequences.

Send thank you notes.

Remember people's birthdays.

Don't talk too long on the phone (he grew up in the days of party lines and when long distance phone calls were expensive).

Wipe out the sink after using it.

Turn the lights off .

If you borrow the car, return it with a full tank of gas.

The neck and giblets are the best parts of the turkey,

Come home from a date at the time that was agreed upon.

When you're upset with someone, go for a walk.

At least once in your life, get up early enough to see the sunrise from a boat on a lake.

If you buy your wife her own computer, she won't be able to delete important files from yours.

Things will last longer if you take care of them.

Saying "You win the Siamese kitten in the contest first, then we'll discuss whether or not you can keep it" might just backfire on you.

After you stay with your grandparents for a week, you have to come back down to earth.

Don't do anything you wouldn't want your parents to find out about.

If you agree to go to the prom with one person, and the next day the person who you really wanted to go to the prom with asks you, you can't go back to the first person and get out of the date. Because if you do, you won't be going to the prom with anyone.

Have an agreement with your wife that you'll take her to any play or concert she wants to see, as long as you can sleep through it.

Pouting will get you nowhere.

It's highly unlikely that you will be the only one going to the dance who's not wearing a new dress.

And finally,

Always keep emergency equipment in your car. My dad left me his car in his will. The other day, under the driver's seat, I found some of his emergency equipment. A carefully folded package containing his grey, plastic rain gear.

LIGHTS, CAMERA, ACTION

Directing the Comedy Readers

There's such a need for humor in the world, and I have lots of friends who are actors in our local community theatre, so I decided to put together a group called the "Comedy Readers." We go to various groups and organizations around town and read jokes and funny stories.

There are about twenty-five of us in our troupe. Usually six of us read at each performance. We don't memorize anything—we simply read from our scripts. Nor do we rehearse together as a group. Everyone gets their scripts and rehearses on their own.

We're pretty good at what we do. Now. But we learned our craft the hard way. When we were first performing, there were several disasters.

Our very first gig was for an all-male breakfast optimist club. We read a short radio play called *The Revenge of the Beauty Operators*, which is a story about a tug of war between two young men and their girlfriends. The play ends with the women outsmarting the men. Even though the audience members were optimists, they didn't think it was very funny.

Another performance we'd like to forget was to a group of ministers' wives. They didn't laugh either. In fact, after we left the room, the person in charge of the program got up and invited everyone to pray for us.

Our third major disaster occurred when we were asked to read at an engagement shower. We'd lost the directions to the house where it was being held, and arrived a little late, so we didn't have a chance to meet our hosts before we began—we just jumped right into our program.

"We're here tonight to celebrate the engagement of Patrick and Susan!"

The bride's mother (who'd hired us, by phone) turned white.

"It's Nancy," someone whispered. "Patrick and Nancy."

I really, really, really, prayed that Patrick's previous girlfriend was not named Susan.

Since then, I'm much more careful about people's names and about matching the pieces we're going to read with the group we're reading for. I file our scripts by category, and select readings based on the main interest of the group (e.g. garden humor for garden clubs, retirement humor for retirement parties, holiday humor for different holidays, etc. etc. etc.) Even that is not enough to ward off all problems so I warn my comedy readers:

1. If someone in the audience falls asleep while you're reading, don't take it personally.
2. If *most* of the audience falls asleep, there's a problem.
3. If someone in the audience is mad at someone else in the audience, and one of them laughs at the joke, you can be assured that the other one (and her friends) won't.
4. At office parties, if the boss (and/or his wife) don't laugh, the employees won't either.

5. Men who laugh at a joke one day may not laugh at it the next day if their wives are present.
6. If the audience doesn't laugh at your punch line, there's no use repeating it in hopes that they will.
7. If the audience isn't laughing, speaking louder won't help.
8. It's hard for the audience to hear when the cleaning lady is vacuuming right outside the room.
9. Groups drinking "hard" beverages laugh more than groups drinking "soft" ones.
10. If you teach your cast to laugh after a piece bombs, sometimes you can fool the audience into thinking it was actually funny.
11. Employees won't laugh, even if it's their annual Christmas party, if they've just been bawled out by their boss for the company's not having a good year.

I'd been an actress before, but never a director. Over the years, I've learned directing is not as easy as it looks. For instance:

1. It's difficult (if not impossible) to direct your friends. Regardless of my extensive experience, brilliant suggestions, and thoughtful planning, they're going to do what they want.
2. Cast members *always* complain that the scripts I've assigned them aren't as funny as the scripts I've given the other members of the cast.
3. Cast members often complain that I haven't asked them to perform as many times as I've asked other people to perform.
4. Even if I send the cast their scripts three weeks in advance, they'll still wait to look at them until the day before the performance at which time they'll call to tell me either (1) they don't like their scripts, or (2) they've rewritten them to make them better, funnier, or longer.

5. I always have a duplicate set of scripts with me. I have one cast member who's a good reader, but when it comes time for him to read, he always fumbles around trying to find the right page. One night, he showed up and told me he didn't want to read one of his scripts because he didn't think it was funny. (He had three to read.) That was fine with me. But I didn't want him to get it confused with his other scripts, so I told him to get rid of it. Unbeknownst to me, he took me literally. He went into the men's room and ripped it into a million little pieces. At that point, a second cast member showed up saying she had left one of her scripts at home on the kitchen table. Of course, that was the one script I didn't bring a spare copy of. So, then I desperately needed Alan's script to make the program long enough. I asked him where his script was. In the men's room. I followed him into the men's room and helped him fish the pieces out of the trash. We sat there, on the floor of the men's room, and furiously scotch-taped the little pieces together while the audience waited patiently for the show to begin.

In spite of these minor challenges, I thoroughly enjoy visiting different groups and organizations around town and bringing them some laughs. And I really enjoy working with this talented group of people. Don't tell them, but I'm not very good at following a director's directions either. In my last show, I repeatedly ignored the director when he told me not to prolong the kiss I had at the end of the play with my leading man.

Right. Like *that* was going to happen.

My Finest, and Not so Fine, Moments in the Theatre

During my first two years in college, I trained to be a professional actress. By the end of my sophomore year, though, I realized there were too many things that would keep me from staring on Broadway.

First, even though my right foot was proficient, my left foot never got the hang of "forward, back, stomp" in tap dancing class.

Second, I couldn't sing.

Third, my height (or lack thereof) limited the parts I was getting. So far, I'd only been cast in children's roles, or as the comedic love interest of very tall men.

Finally, it was highly unlikely that my conservative parents would support me while I went off to try my luck in New York.

So I changed majors.

To satisfy my love of the stage, I became active in our local community theatre. It took me awhile to get used to the differences between community theatre and professional theatre. Instead of having paid employees, community theatres are dependent on volunteers (who can't always make it to rehearsals because they have to work late or take their kids to soccer practice). Rehearsals in a theatre program are serious; rehearsals in a community theatre are much more laid-back. In our community theatre, for example, the routine was: you showed up for rehearsals (as often as you could), practiced for a few hours, and then went out to drink at the local pub.

One thing both professional and amateur theatres *do* have in common is that there are always misadventures. As I look back on some of my experiences onstage, I can recall some moments where I'm extremely proud of my behavior, and some where I'm not so proud.

So, get ready to take a quiz. I'm going to describe six scenarios (aka tense moments) from plays I've been in. Read them and decide which category they fall into—a moment I should be proud of, or a moment I probably shouldn't be proud of.

You're going to either vote "bravo" or "boo."

SCENARIO #1:

In a production of *Never Too Late*, I was playing the daughter, Kate. In one scene, the actress playing my mother and I had an intimate mother-daughter dialogue. We got through it just fine in rehearsals, but on opening night, after I said my line, Doris got a blank look on her face. Now, there's nothing quite as exciting as being onstage with someone who forgets their next line. If you're not careful, it can easily become a scene where you both forget your lines and you have to stand there until one of you thinks of something to say or the stage manager closes the curtain.

When your co-star forgets her line, the first thing you do is ask yourself: "What's happening here?" Did she really forget her line, or is she just taking a dramatic pause? After you've let the dramatic pause go on and still nothing comes out of her mouth, you realize you need to do something.

Now, I'm not quick on my feet, so I usually wait until someone else onstage gets us out of our mess. But in this case, we were the only two in the scene. Since this was Doris's first acting experience, I figured it was going to be up to me to save the scene. My adrenaline clicked in, and I said: "Oh, mom, I'll bet you're going to tell me ..." and then proceeded to say *her* line.

Doris's pupils opened a little wider, but she remained mute. So

I said *my* next line and paused. Still no response. So then I said HER next line: "Oh, mom, I'll bet you're going to tell me ..." And that's how we got through the scene. I said both my lines and hers.

When the scene ended and the lights went down, I took her by the hand, walked her offstage, and turned her over to the stage manager. I don't know what happened after that. I think someone gave her a shot of whiskey.

So, was that a moment I should be proud of? Or not so proud of? You're right. Proud moment. A bravo for me.

Bravo __X__ Boo_____

That was fairly easy. Try this next one.

SCENARIO #2:

I was playing Essie in a production of *You Can't Take it with You*. Essie is one of the most fun parts ever written. You're on stage most of the time, you can be cute and perky, you don't have many lines, and you're not responsible for the show being a success or a failure.

In the opening scene, Essie flits around with a tray of candy, offering the candy to everyone onstage. Dialogue is exchanged. Another actor enters the scene. Only during one performance, that actor didn't enter the scene. What happens then is that the remaining actors have to start ad-libbing to fill the blank space created by that character's absence. "How do you like this weather?" "Jolly good weather, old chap. Jolly good." Stuff like that. The problem is: the more you ad lib, the less likely it is that the person offstage will appear. Actors are programmed to come on only when they hear their cue. So, what happened was, the stage manager, who was backstage reading from the script and having a heart attack, had to run over from the other side of the stage which, in our case, wasn't easy because he had to go outdoors and come in another stage door (which was locked so latecomers couldn't walk out onstage during a performance), and push the actor out onstage.

Well, I had ad-libbed my heart out, and the scene was going downhill fast. My fight or flight instinct took over. I picked up my tray, announced to the other characters onstage: "I'm going to the kitchen to make some more candy," and exited.

I wish I could say I exited to go find the actor and send him out onstage. That wasn't it. I just wanted to get out of there.

Your turn.

Bravo _____ Boo_____

SCENARIO #3:

In a production of *Crossing Delancey*, I was cast as the lead, Izzy. When I accepted the role, I knew it was a fairly big part. Once we got into rehearsals, I discovered it was a huge part. Izzy is on stage practically the whole play, except for the times when she's frantically changing her clothes in the wings. (Note to future thespians: read the entire play before you accept a part.)

Besides having to deal with the stressful costume changes, I had to look good (also stressful), and remember to do a Jewish accent, which was difficult because there weren't a lot of Jewish accents in our town that I could copy. The success of the show fell directly on my shoulders. At night, when I'd go to bed, I'd dream I was pushing a large bolder up a hill.

Of all the challenges I had, the biggest one was getting myself in place—in the dark—for the opening of one of the scenes. The thing is: Not only can I not see in the dark, I have no depth perception. Wearing a tight skirt and high heels, I was expected to step up onto an eight inch platform. To manage that maneuver, I had to pull my skirt up, bend my knee and lift my right leg as high as I could. If I didn't lift my leg high enough, I'd hit the toe of my shoe on the platform and fall flat on my face. Which I did once at a rehearsal. So, I'd stand there in the dark, lifting my right leg and pawing the air like a horse trying to find the platform. Luckily the lighting guys could see me and knew not to turn the lights up until I got in place.

In addition to having nightmares about the show and not being able to see in the dark, I started having trouble with my contact lenses. My left contact felt fine, but my right contact felt scratchy, like there was sand in my eye. So, for the last several performances, I wore just my left contact lens. Now, there was a huge difference between the vision in my left eye (with the contact lens), and my right eye (where everything was one big blur). To see the character I was talking to, I had to tilt my head to the right and look out of my left eye. To make eye contact with me, my fellow actors had to tilt their heads as well.

I'm going to stop the story here. It's time for you to vote. I'll give you a third option on this one:

Bravo _____ Boo_____ Just Plain Pathetic_____

SCENARIO #4:

Neil Simon's play *Plaza Suite* has a wonderful part for an actress, like me, who wants to be important to the story, yet not have very many lines to remember. I was playing the part of Mimsey, a young bride on her wedding day, who locks herself in the bathroom of her room at the Plaza hotel and won't come out. The humor in the scene comes from the different ways her parents try to get her to come out. The scene is funny and very well written, and the actors playing the parents in our production were superb.

Throughout the scene, "Dad" calls through the bathroom door, bangs on it, and tries to turn the door knob to get his daughter out. Nothing works. At the end of the play, the groom shows up, and says "Mimsey? ... This is Borden ... Cool it!" Mimsey promptly appears, says "I'm ready now," and exits. The father exits also, a wreck after the ordeal he's been through.

Well, it seemed ridiculous to me to spend an hour sitting backstage on a folding chair (in a heavy wedding gown), so, after I put my makeup on, I'd sneak out into the back of the theatre and watch the show along with the audience. About fifteen minutes before my entrance, I'd race backstage, jump into the wedding dress, and listen for my cue.

This worked fine until the night when, in the middle of the scene, "Dad" pushed too hard on the bathroom door and it flew open. With me not behind it.

It was obvious to those of us in the audience there was no bride in the bathroom. Where was she? How did she disappear? There's no play without the bride locking herself in the bathroom. I sat there horrified. The audience seemed confused. The actor playing my father was the one who was the most surprised. Luckily, he had the presence of mind to quickly pull the door shut and yell: "Oh, my God! She's locked the door again!!"

I was just a volunteer. Could they fire me if I was just a volunteer?

For the rest of the performances, I dutifully sat backstage in the heavy dress on the hard, folding chair and waited for my entrance.

Bravo _____ Boo_____

SCENARIO #5:

Dial M for Murder is a classic murder mystery. I was cast in the role of Margot, the part that Grace Kelly played in the movie. It was another perfect part for me—there were several scenes I wasn't in, so I could go down to the dressing room, put my feet up, and have a beer.

In a murder mystery, props are essential. You must have the right props, at the right time, in the right place. For this particular play, raincoats and keys were critical.

Our first three performances (of nine) went fine, but disaster struck on our fourth. Margot opens Act II, scene three nervously pacing the floor, sipping a cup of coffee. After a few sips, Tony, her husband, enters. Only on this night, he didn't.

Normally, Tony appeared after I'd had about three sips. This night, I paced and sipped. Paced and sipped. Paced and sipped. I finished the cup of coffee. I poured another one. Paced and sipped. Paced and sipped. My heart was pounding. I was frantic. Where was Tony? I finished my second cup of coffee. Where was Tony?

I was pouring my third cup as slowly as I could when I heard the door finally open. I opened my mouth to say my first line. Only it wasn't Tony. It was a young man I'd never seen before, dressed entirely in black. He came tiptoeing onstage, hunched over (like he didn't want to be seen), carrying Tony's raincoat. He hung the coat on the coat rack and "sneaked" out the center stage door. The audience and I watched him in absolute amazement.

Obviously he was a stage hand, and obviously we needed the raincoat for the scene to go on. But what if I'd said my line to him? What if I'd said my line to him? Would he have stopped and answered back?

As soon as he exited, Tony appeared and we began the scene. At the end of the scene, I raced to the bathroom to get rid of all the coffee I'd had.

You *have* to give me this one.

Bravo __X__ Boo_____

SCENARIO #6:

In our production of *Philadelphia Story*, I was cast as Liz, the newspaper photographer. Another wonderful part. I was an important character, got to wear flattering costumes, got kissed every night, and my lines were easy to remember. I was having a great time in rehearsals, although I was a bit bothered by the fact that my fellow thespians didn't always stay in character.

Especially when Freddie was onstage.

Freddie was one of those people who enjoyed getting his fellow actors to start laughing. During rehearsals, he'd do things like come onstage carrying props that weren't in our show, or playing his part with an Australian accent. Every night it was something different. He could get everyone to break up. Except me. I was trained to stay in character no matter what happened.

The rehearsal the night before we opened was particularly tense. There were problems with the lights, problems with sound, and problems with the set changes. Actors couldn't remember their lines and were still breaking character. The director had had it—especially with the cast. He came into our dressing rooms at intermission and threatened to kick us out of the show if any of us broke character in the final scene—Freddie's favorite scene to pull a joke in.

After the director's little "talk," we were all nervous about Freddie's entrance. We braced ourselves for his pulling something again. And he did.

He entered with the legs of his tuxedo rolled up to his knees.

I don't know why, but it hit me as funny. I smiled. Somehow the smile grew into a giggle. The giggle grew into a laugh. Then, once I started laughing, I couldn't stop. The laughter I'd kept inside during all those weeks of rehearsal erupted. I threw my head back and laughed loudly. I hugged my stomach and doubled over laughing. I was laughing so hard I had to reach out and steady myself on another actor. After that, I collapsed, laughing, onto the floor. From there, I rolled up into a fetal position, banged my fists on the floor with tears flowing from my eyes, and howled in delightful ecstasy.

Everybody else, staying perfectly in character, just stared at me. They finished the scene by stepping over me and saying my lines for me.

Deeply embarrassed, I sneaked out the back door of the theatre knowing I was going to need to apologize to everyone—especially the director—the next night.

Bravo _____ Boo_____

Now, using the following scale, tally up your answers.

6 Bravos ___ You think I'm ready to star on Broadway.

5 Bravos ___ You'd pay money to see me.

4 Bravos ___ You'd come to see me if someone gave you a free ticket.

3 Bravos ___ You wouldn't come to see me—even with a free ticket.

2 Bravos ___ You'd discourage people you like from coming to see me.

1 Bravo ___ You'd discourage people you dislike from coming to see me.

All Boos ___ I should avoid the theatre. Even as an audience member.

Shooting the Cover of My Book

When my book *The Misadventures of a Single Woman* was being edited, my publisher asked me what I wanted on the cover. I had two ideas: a picture of a beautiful young girl standing in a field of colorful flowers, or something funny that would depict the theme of the book: "misadventures."

I consulted with my creative friend, Tom.

"The cover of your book? You should wear a long dress and stand in the rain looking all soggy with your hair plastered to your head."

"Tom, I'm not going to do that. Besides, we need to shoot it this weekend. What if it doesn't rain?"

He had an answer for that.

"Okay. Have someone stand behind you with a garden hose, spraying you with water."

Although that picture *would* represent many of the relationships I've had with men, I decided to go with my idea of a beautiful young girl in a field of flowers. I didn't have a beautiful young girl, so I decided I could be the model if I wore a hat down over my face. Nor did I have a field of colorful flowers, but they shouldn't be hard to find. Luckily, I did have a photographer. I could enlist my significant other, Sam, to shoot the picture.

How hard could shooting a picture be?

The first problem I encountered was that I couldn't fit into the white dress I'd planned to wear. The one from a long time ago. I could get it on, but it would only zip up to my waist. Solution: I'd have Sam photograph me only from the front.

The second problem was that we didn't have a garden full of

flowers. Solution: there was a garden close to campus. When Sam and I went over to investigate, we found a field of magnificent, waist-high, purple irises. I could stand in the middle of them. It would be the perfect spot for a picture.

Which we decided to shoot that weekend.

On Saturday morning, I put on the dress and zipped it as far up as it would go. The flowered hat I wanted to wear was too big for my head, so I went to my closet and dug out an old wig. The wig was hot and heavy, but it made the hat fit, so I wore it. To add a touch of "funky," I wore a knee-high pair of leather boots.

Sam picked me up and we drove over to the garden. To our dismay, the roads surrounding the garden were blocked off due to construction. The closest we could park was four blocks away, then we had to tramp through the dirty, dusty, construction site. It was slow tramping because of my long dress and winter boots. Sam didn't want the construction workers to see my back (what was there to see?) so he walked next to me holding the back of my dress together. This was probably a lot more conspicuous than if I'd just walked by myself.

Anyway, we arrived at the garden, I stood in the middle of the spectacular purple irises, and Sam shot some pictures. We sent them off to the publisher.

Who loved them. He called Sam on the phone, though, and asked him to reshoot the picture using a "raw" setting (whatever that is). Sam seemed to know. Also, instead of shooting the picture vertically, he wanted it shot horizontally, with me in the right hand side of the frame so that he could wrap some of the garden scene around to the back cover.

No problem.

The book was almost ready to go to press, so the publisher needed the picture as soon as possible. Unfortunately, it rained that whole next week, but on the first sunny day, Sam and I went back to the garden to reshoot the picture. Once again, I donned the white dress (zipped up as much as possible), the wig, the hat, and the winter boots.

This time, Sam was determined to park in front of the garden so we wouldn't have to walk through the construction site. To do that, he drove down a blocked-off street in the wrong direction (which I guess didn't matter since it was blocked off), around a series of orange barriers, and up onto the sidewalk.

When we pulled up to the curb, we were horrified. The purple irises were gone. Gone!

Had someone stolen them? Had a runaway bulldozer from the construction site plowed them under? Then it dawned on us. The heavy winds from the storms the previous week must have wiped them out.

Now what?

We returned to my house where I changed my clothes, and we set out to find a garden with colorful flowers. I began by calling Isobel. Did any of the members of her garden club have flowers? They didn't. We drove to a nursery across town. Maybe they'd have a display of flowers I could stand in. They didn't. We asked the manager of the nursery if he knew of any gardens that might have survived the storms. He didn't. We got back in the car and started driving around town, looking in people's yards for colorful flowers. No luck.

It was now mid-afternoon. We had to shoot the picture while there was still some sun. In desperation, we went to Wal-Mart, bought $40 worth of flowers, and loaded them into the back of Sam's SUV. My friend Linda offered to loan us three hanging baskets of pansies she had on her back porch. We swung by her house and picked them up, along with a small stool. We could use the stool, Linda thought, to hold some of the Wal-Mart flowers up off the ground. We returned to my house where I got back into my white dress.

By now, it was hot. The flowers were already starting to droop.

We drove to the gardens (in the same illegal way) and unloaded the flowers in the area where the irises used to be. Sam was able to carry two planters of flowers at a time (one in each hand), but I could only carry one since I had to use the other hand to hold up the top of my dress. We hung Linda's baskets of hanging flowers on the fence in the background and set some of the Wal-Mart flowers on Linda's stool. The entire time, we were watching for the police in case they drove by and saw that we were trampling down what was left of the purple irises. If the police caught us, I was going to say we'd brought the flowers from Wal-Mart in an effort to help beautify the community. I had no idea how I was going to explain being in the white dress.

We began taking pictures. Every so often, Sam would bring his camera over to where I was standing so I could view them in the view finder. We shot picture after picture. Then we shot some more pictures. One hundred and ten pictures later, I was satisfied we had enough. We reloaded our flowers into the back of Sam's SUV and went to his house to view the pictures on his computer.

"Make a list of the ones you don't want," Sam instructed, handing me a pen and a little notebook. So I began critiquing them. Right arm too high. Left arm too low. Wrong angle on the hat. Shadow across my face. Mouth shaped funny. Not enough flowers. Bicycle rider in the background. Didn't look joyful enough. Arms looked like I was being held up in a bank robbery.

I eliminated all 110.

"We have to do it again," I said. Sam took his glasses off and rubbed his face.

The next day we repeated the procedure. Put the dress on. Drove down the street illegally. Parked illegally. Unloaded the flowers (which were now really drooping) from the back of the SUV. Tried to remember where we'd put the flowers the previous day. Sam remembered them in certain positions. I went around and moved them to where they were supposed to be.

This time, I decided to go for a whole new look. Wanting to look even more joyous than before, I decided to kick my leg out to the side while throwing my arms up in the air. But it was hot. Very, very hot. And humid. Very, very humid. Sam and I were wet and sweaty before we even started taking pictures.

Imagine standing on a hot summer day in a flower bed wearing a hot wig, heavy winter boots, and a dress that's too tight, while kicking your leg out to the side and throwing your hands up in the air. With a photographer who had already done this two other times and who thought the previous pictures were good enough.

Every few pictures we'd stop, and Sam would walk over and show them to me.

"We don't have it yet," I said. Sam took his glasses off and rubbed his face.

My dress was soaked. After each shot, Sam and I would stop and wipe our faces off with a towel. But we had to get the shot.

"I think we have it this time," Sam said after a few more shots. I looked in the viewfinder. No. My left arm needed to be higher. I wanted to try kicking my right leg out instead of my left. Maybe I should take a step back and be closer to the fence.

After about the ninety-ninth shot, I had heat stroke. Sam walked me over to the car and turned the air conditioning on. I unzipped my dress so I could breathe, took my wig off, drank some water, and fanned myself with the hat.

"I'm sure we have it by now," he said.

"Let's take a few more."

We ended up taking one hundred and seventy-two shots. This time, I didn't look at them. I sent them all off to the publisher. Who, upon reviewing them, sent me this note:

"Hi, Sally: Pix are great!!! We selected one."

Jim has a great sense of humor, so I wrote back:

Dear Jim: Does the picture you selected capture the fact that the dress was two sizes too small, that we'd had storms here so there weren't any flowers left in the garden, that we had to buy flowers at Wal-Mart to put on the ground, that the humidity was 90%, that the wig I was wearing was hot and heavy, that I was wearing my winter boots, that I was sweating like a pig, and that we'd parked illegally and had to tramp through a bunch of construction to get to the site?"

"Yep."

Joining the Church Choir

Our church was having its annual drive to recruit new members for the various committees. As usual, during this period of time, I was keeping a low profile. I was careful to be the last person to arrive at the Sunday morning service, and the first person to leave so no one could nab me.

My plan was working fine until Annie Lou, a colleague of mine at work, called. I knew instantly what she was calling about. Shoot! What excuse could I give her for why I couldn't be on her church growth committee? Thinking quickly, I said:

"I'd love to be on your committee, Annie Lou, but I've decided to join the choir. One night a week at church is all I can handle. Sorry."

Instead of saying: "Thanks, anyway. Bye," she said:

"Fantastic! We rehearse tomorrow at seven. Tell you what—I'll swing by and pick you up."

Now, when I said I'd decided to join the choir, I'd meant eventually. Not any time soon.

As I sat there kicking myself, I began to think of reasons why joining the choir might not be such a bad idea. I'd always wanted to learn to sing—this could be a chance to get some free lessons. The choir robes were brilliant blue. I looked good in blue. The choir was a well-respected, well-oiled machine. Even if I didn't know what I was doing, there were so many of them, my inexperience wouldn't be noticed.

And the best part was: everybody in church—from the minister on down—would see that I was contributing.

The choir members welcomed me enthusiastically when I

appeared the next night at their rehearsal. The choir secretary handed me a stack of sheet music. The person in charge of the robes assigned me a robe. Robe #17. How cool was that? The previous robe #17 wearer must have been a lot taller than me, but I didn't care. He was gone. I was now choir member #17.

The director came over and asked me what part I sang. I had no idea. Whenever I have occasion to sing, I always sing an octave lower than the main melody, but I was reluctant to say that in case there was some sort of rule in the music business that you weren't supposed to sing an octave lower.

"We need altos," she said. "Let's start you as an alto."

Oh-Kay. I went and sat on the folding chairs over with the altos.

We began by humming for a while to warm up our voices. Then we "la'ed" up and down the scale: " La la la la la la la la la."

Then we "ah'ed": "ah, ah, ah, ah, ah, ah, ah."

Then we practiced our enunciation: "me may ma mo moo. Me, may, ma, mo, moo." Then we did some sirens, which is where you make the sound of a fire truck going to the scene of an accident. I was right in there humming, sirening and "la, la-ing" along with everybody else. It was great fun. I sounded good. I should have done this years ago.

Then we got to our first song: "What a friend we have in Jesus." I knew that one. No, I didn't. What I knew was the soprano part, not the alto part. While the sopranos were singing the melody, we altos had to stand there and sing five "F's" in a row. How exciting was that? Not.

Having boring notes to sing was the least of my worries. I was having trouble reading the music. The notes were at the top of the page, but the lyrics were about half an inch farther down. How was I supposed to read both of those things at the same time? Suddenly I noticed no one else was even referring to their music. They'd sung it so many times they knew the notes—and the lyrics—by heart.

My next challenge had to do with timing. When I pound out show tunes on my piano at home, I pound them out at my own speed. I quickly realized that in a choir, they expect everyone to go at the same speed. This means you have to pay really close attention to the little dots and flags that tell you how long to hold the notes. Meanwhile, you're expected to watch the director. I was making all sorts of mistakes—starting to sing before everyone else, and continuing to sing after everyone else had stopped. It only took a few times of doing that for me to learn to start singing after everyone else did and stop before everyone else did.

Next I discovered I didn't know how to breathe. We'd moved on to "Holy, Holy, Holy," and the director wanted us to sing the line: "Holy, holy, holy, Lord God almighty, Early in the morning, our song shall rise to Thee" before we took our first breath. I was gasping for breath after my first three "Holy, holy, holy's." I gestured to the accompanist to pick the pace up. She smiled at me like you would at someone from another planet who you wouldn't want to make mad.

The next thing I learned was that I couldn't find the notes on my own. Yes, I could read the note on the page, and yes, I could hear the note in my head, but by the time it came out of my mouth, it was an entirely different sound. What I did was, move closer to the alto on my right and wait until she got the note. Then I copied her. She didn't seem to mind, but there wasn't much she could do. She was up against the wall and couldn't get away.

Rehearsal ended. I realized I was in over my head.

I took the sheet music for our anthem home so I could practice it. I practiced that darned song all week.

Sunday morning arrived. It was exciting to put on my own robe

(robe #17) there alongside all the other choir members. I stuck my chest out, proud to be a part of this well-respected, well-oiled machine. As we marched down the aisle singing our introit, I held my open hymnal in one hand, and the bottom of my too-long choir robe in the other. Since I wasn't able to find the key notes on my own, I walked smack dab up against the choir member in front of me so I could copy the notes she was singing.

We entered the choir loft, and I took a seat between the two altos I'd rehearsed next to. But we'd only rehearsed in the choir room, not in the sanctuary. Now that I was there, I couldn't help but notice we were packed in like sardines.

Everything was going fine. The minister greeted the congregation and made some announcements. There were some readings from the Bible. They took the collection. They had the children's sermon. It was time now for our anthem.

The choir director got up from her chair, which was off to the side, and positioned herself in front of us. She put her foot on the base of her music stand and raised it to the right height for her music. She gave us a matronly smile, and then raised her arms to indicate that we should stand.

Well, I was so excited, I was the first one on my feet. As I stood up, I opened my black folder that contained my music. Now, in my own defense, let me repeat that we were packed in there like sardines. In the process of jumping to my feet and opening my black folder, I managed to bump the lady's head in front of me, which caused her to drop her folder. Her music scattered all over the floor. The people on either side of her bent down to help her pick it up, but, again, these were pretty tight quarters. Everyone who bent down displaced the person next to them, so everyone had to adjust. I felt terrible, so I immediately leaned down to apologize. In doing so, I somehow managed to bump into the alto on my right, causing her to drop *her* folder.

The alto on my left gasped so loudly (nothing like this had ever happened since she'd joined the choir one hundred years ago) that I swung around to apologize to her. But she must not have expected me to, or else she didn't have a very good hold onto her folder, because down it went down, too.

That's when I decided to hold perfectly still.

I remember shooting a glance at the choir director. She stood frozen—from head to foot—with her arms poised in midair. I remember wondering if her face would ever be able to relax out of that position.

Anyway, everyone picked up their music and we made it through the anthem. And through the service.

I stuck with the choir for about four months. I'd like to say things got better, but they didn't. After that, I was careful about the way I stood up when we were in the choir loft, but I never did learn how to sing.

The choir gave me a potluck, carry-in lunch on the last Sunday I sang with them. At first I thought they had going-away parties for everyone who left the choir, but nope. It was just for me.

There is some good news: since then, nobody's asked me to be on another church committee.

BRINGING HOME THE BACON

What I Like About My Job

As a single career woman, my job has always been important to me. At the end of a work day, I get a great deal of satisfaction in knowing I've done my best, and that I'm making a difference in the world.

Every job has its own positives and negatives, pluses and minuses, and ups and downs. Here are the aspects of my job I enjoy the most and that make it special to me.

First, I can park close to my office. That's a plus. As soon as I get out of my car in the morning, my heart starts racing. That's because I park in a parking garage and people come pealing through at ninety miles an hour and don't look where they're going.

Our office family is like the Waltons. In the morning, when we come in, we all say "good morning" to each other. "Good morning, Juan." " Good morning, Chuck." "Good morning, Deb." "Good morning, David." Then, in the evening, when we leave, we say good night. "Good night." "Have a good one." "Have a good evening." "See you tomorrow." In between our "hellos" and "goodbye's," we try to avoid each other as much as possible.

Morale in our office is high, if measured by attendance. Mostly, though, we come to work because the vacation forms and sick leave forms are too complicated to fill out.

This may have nothing to do with morale, but a year ago, they came through and sealed up our windows so we can't open them.

The chair that goes with my desk is really fancy. It came with a six-page book of instructions on how to adjust it. I've never been able to figure out how it works, but it's black leather and looks really sharp.

My office is close to the women's restroom. Another plus. But it can be dangerous to go in there. The paper towel machine has a sign on it that says "Tirez avec les deux mains" which means "if you want a paper towel, you're going to have to smack me with your fist." The machine is next to the door, so when you stand there smacking it, you run the risk of being decked when someone—who's waited until the last minute—comes barreling in.

There are brochures in the front office that tell visitors what we do. I go down and read them periodically to see if what I'm supposed to be doing has changed.

Daniel is our business manager. He's a really neat guy, and he'd like to give us all the money he could, but they've trained him to never say the word "yes." I've seen him try on several occasions, but what happens is that he starts choking, his hands fly up to his throat, and it looks like he's trying to do a self-Heimlich maneuver.

Jimmy Johns is right down the street. They have great sandwiches which they deliver right to our offices. This is especially handy when we have to eat lunch at our desks because the boss has told us at 11:45 that she wants us to write an annual report of everything we did the past year and turn it in by 5:00.

We have lots of meetings. We even had a meeting on how to fill out the form to schedule the room for meetings.

The chairs in the conference room can be adjusted up and down ... and they swivel. Sometimes, while we're waiting for the staff meeting to begin, we try to see how many times we can spin around.

When my computer tells me I'm late for a meeting, I can erase the screen with a flick of the delete button. Poof! That annoying little message is gone.

We have access to an unlimited supply of little, yellow post-it notes. I'm not sure what they're for, but I always take one to the staff meetings in case sometime, somebody says something I might want to write down.

Recently, our building deputy instituted a recycling program. We have new, state-of-the-art wastepaper baskets in our offices which are divided into two sections—one for "office paper," and one for "recyclables." We're supposed to take our "trash" down the hall to a big green trash bin in our break room.

There was a training session to teach us how to distinguish between "office paper," "recyclables," and "trash." We had a lot of questions:

"Does the paper we put in the 'office paper' side have to be 8 ½" by 11"? What if it's smaller than that?"

"Or larger?"

"What if it's colored?"

"What if it's wadded up? Do we need to flatten it out?"

"What if it's shiny?"

"What if it's wadded up and shiny?"

The trainers gave up trying to explain "office paper" and moved on to "recyclables" and "trash." The topic of empty yogurt containers came up. According to them, yogurt containers could go one of two places, depending on how much yogurt was left in the container. A yogurt container with less than 10% residue would go into the "recyclable" side of our office wastepaper basket. A yogurt container with more than 10% of the yogurt left in it would go down the hall into the "trash."

We were confused. They could tell we were confused.

Instead of finishing the session, the trainers decided it would be easier to just put labels (listing what goes where) on the wastepaper baskets.

Speaking of food, sometimes there's food in the main office. It's usually left-over from someone's meeting.

"Did you get that out of the trash can?"

"It was still in a box ..."

Safety is a major concern in our building. Luckily, we have state-of-the-art alarms to warn us about tornadoes and fires. When we hear the fire alarm, we're supposed to take the stairs and exit the building. When we hear the tornado alarm, we're supposed to go all the way down to the basement. Unfortunately, the two alarms sound alike, so the two groups of people—those going outside, and those going to the basement—meet on the main floor and create a huge traffic jam so no one can go anyplace.

And finally, our offices all have artwork on the walls. In my office, there's a beautiful poster of an old-fashioned bicycle leaning against a French pastry shop. I suspect it was put there to help me focus on my work.

Instead, it makes me think: "Man, I'd really like to be on that bicycle right now."

Seeing My Book for the First Time

When my publisher called to tell me my book had been printed and that he was sending me one in the mail, I raced down the block to Von's bookstore to ask Jim, the manager, if I could have my first book signing there.

Throughout the years, I'd bought a lot of books at Von's, but had never had a conversation with Jim before. I was nervous. Instead of rushing in out of breath, I stopped and checked my hair in the window. Then, calmly and professionally (as author-like as I could), I entered the store.

Jim was at his typewriter. Yes, typewriter. Jim doesn't use a computer—he types on an old-fashioned typewriter. I told him about my book and asked if I could have a book signing there. He continued typing. Then, without looking up, said: "I guess we could." I interpreted that as a sign of wild excitement on his part. We agreed on a date.

Now, let me back up a minute and tell you about Von's. Von's is the most wonderful, old-fashioned bookstore in the world. *Everybody* goes to Von's. We locals go, and whenever we have out-of-town guests, Von's is one of the first places we take them.

It's in an old brick building close to the university campus. To your right, when you enter the store, there's an old, wooden desk. That's where you pay for your books. If someone is standing there buying a book and you want to get around them, you have to squeeze by. The same with the aisles. When you're browsing the shelves for books, there's very little room to maneuver. Who cares? The shelves are packed with books from floor to ceiling with every book you could want. The books aren't covered with dust. But for just a second, imagine they were, and you'd have a feel for the store.

After you pass through the bookstore, you walk up a ramp and enter an enchanting room filled with exotic gifts—beaded necklaces, ankle bracelets, incense, rocks, and oriental boxes. If you walk through that room, you enter a third room—the music room. CDs, DVDs, and old posters are watched over by a young hippie with long hair and a tie-dyed shirt who knows everything you'd want to know about music.

What's special about Von's is that when you go in, you're immediately transported to another world. The 1960s. They're not trying to be retro. They just haven't changed anything since the sixties.

Jim, the quintessential bookstore manager, is as unique as the store. Somewhere between the ages of thirty and one hundred, he looks like your typical absent-minded professor. And he knows where every book in the store is.

Now, Jim is a man of few words. When you go in and ask for a book, he gets up, finds it, hands it to one of his employees, and returns to his typewriter.

Okay. Back to my story. Jim and I set a date for my book signing and I left.

Several days later, while I was waiting for my book to arrive in the mail, I stopped in at Von's to browse. As always, Jim was working at his typewriter. He saw me and said in his quiet, unassuming manner: "Your book just came in."

"My book came in? It did? Oh, my gosh! Can I see it? I haven't seen it yet!" He had to open several boxes before he found the box that contained my book. Then, in his quiet, matter-of-fact way, he handed me the one on top. I took it, touched the cover, and immediately started crying.

"It's so small!" I cried.

Jim had already started heading back to his typewriter. He stopped.

"No, it's not," he said awkwardly. "It's the right size for a book. It's fine."

I kept crying.

"I didn't mean to make you cry." Customers were looking over at us.

"Oh, that's all right," I said. "Men have been making me cry my whole life. That's what the book is about."

I wiped my nose on my sleeve. "Do you have a Kleenex?"

The gal in a long hippie skirt standing behind the desk said: "We don't have Kleenex, but we have a roll of toilet paper." She reached under her desk and handed it to me.

So there I stood, holding a roll of toilet paper, and blowing my nose. Customers had now gathered to see what was going on.

Jim apologized again. "I'm sorry I made you cry."

"Oh. That's all right. I cried when my dentist retired. And I hardly knew him."

Jim tried again. "Go ahead and keep that copy if you want."

"Oh, no," I said, handing it back, along with the roll of toilet paper. "I don't want to lose the royalty."

Back at my office, I propped my feet up on my desk and pondered my new role in life. I was now an author. A published author. Hey. I'd be getting a royalty check. What should I do with my first royalty check?

It would be nice to get the drippy faucet in my bathroom sink fixed.

And while the plumber was there, I could have him install a new shower head. The holes in my shower head are plugged up and when I take a shower, instead of the water coming straight down like it should, it shoots out sideways and hits me in the face. Definitely a new shower head.

Hey. I could get the lock on my back door fixed. In its current state, I have to use both hands to unlock the door. With my left hand, I pull the knob towards me—but not all the way. Only about ninety-two percent of the way. Then, with my right hand, I have to turn the key in the lock with just the right amount of pressure and at a forty-five degree angle. Not forty-four. Not forty-six. Forty-five. And both of these movements must be done in sync with each other. While I'm struggling with the door, I can see my cats (through the window) sitting on the kitchen floor making bets on how long it will take.

It sure would be nice to get a new lock.

Then, I'd put the rest of the money in the bank.

Wait. The next time Scotty cut my hair, I could let her style it (which costs more money) instead of leaving the salon with my hair still wet.

"Let me blow dry your hair," she always offers.

"No, that's all right," I lie. "I *like* wet hair. I'm not doing anything else today. I'll be fine." (Grab my coat and run out the door while everyone stares at me out the front window.)

Oh. Oh. Oh. Here's one! I'd love to pay full price for a sweatshirt instead of buying them at Goodwill. Sweatshirts are usually pretty worn out by the time they get to Goodwill. Oh! And I want it to have lettering. Embossed lettering. I don't care what the letters say; I just want it to have embossed lettering.

Then, I'd put the rest of the money in the bank.

Although, if I had some extra money, I wouldn't have to stand at the post office and debate whether to send a package first class or priority mail when the difference is only forty cents.

And I could buy two—no, three—no, four rolls of paper towels at the same time.

I could buy my own pen instead of taking a handful of pens every time I went to the bank.

I could stop turning greeting cards over to see the price before buying them.

I could buy a kitchen knife. That cut. I could start using recipes that involved cutting things up.

Oh my gosh! I could buy an umbrella that stayed open by itself. I could throw away the one I have now that I have to hold open with my thumb. Holy cow! I could buy *two* umbrellas. Then I could have one in my car and one here at home. Wait! What I *really* want is one of those see-through umbrellas that covers your head and neck and comes down all the way to your shoulders.

Then, I'd put the rest of the money in the bank.

But, wouldn't it be nice to buy a bottle of expensive hairspray that wouldn't make my hand stick to my hair when I've checked to see if I've sprayed enough?

Here's one. I'd like to take everyone who's currently in the military, has ever been in the military, or has ever contributed to the effort of any of the wars we fought in, to Disneyworld to thank them for making it possible for me to be a single woman, to live in a safe country, and to create my own life.

One last thing. I'd like to go to Von's and buy a best-selling book when it first comes out instead of waiting months for it to come in at the library.

Just think! I could buy a hardback copy of MY book instead of waiting for it to come out in paperback.

Then ... I'd put the rest of the money in the bank.

My First Fan Letter

Kitty Kimball-Campbell
21206 Little Potato Creek Road
Sebring, IL 12345

Dear Sara Jane: (May I call you Sara Jane?)

*Y*ou don't know me, but I'm a writer, too! I loved your book ... especially the fact that you got it published. I'm writing to get your advice on how I can get MY book, *My Life, Take it or Leave it*, published. Since you're a published author, I'm hoping that you'll have it in your heart to help me, a struggling young writer.

First of all, everyone tells me to get an agent, but I figure: why let someone get 15% of my profit when I can edit my book myself? The way I see it, if you can write, you can edit. I'll admit, I'm not the world's best speller or punctuator (is that a word?), but—hello—isn't that the job of the copy editor at the publishing company?

You know what I think? Here's what I think. Sometimes I think publishers don't even read what I send them. It's like they have someone screening their mail. Plus, it really makes me mad that after all the work I put into my manuscript (plus the postage to mail it) they reject it without telling me WHY. Do you think that's fair? I don't think that's fair.

I've done my research and, according to *The Writer's Market*, publishers want writers to send their manuscripts to only one publishing company at a time. Are they nuts? Who would do that? (As you can infer, I don't follow that rule. Besides, how would anybody even know if I've sent something to more than one publishing company at a time? Ha!)

Those are just some of my thoughts. Now I have some questions:

QUESTION #1: According to *The Writer's Market*, there's a publishing company in New York City (in New York) that's "actively seeking books on Appalachia." I was thinking: maybe I could just add the word "Appalachia" to the title of my book. I could call it *My Life, Take it or Leave it IN APPALACHIA*! Instead of working "in the restaurant business" (aka a truck stop), I could say I worked in a coal mine. I could change the locations in the book from the real ones to ones in West Virginia that I find on MapQuest. Do you think that would work?

There's another company that's looking for books in the categories of "humor, horse training, and Internet marketing." Do you suppose they're looking for books that contain all three of those things? Really? I was thinking I could tell them that my book HAS all of those things and then worry about putting horses and internet marketing stuff in after they say they want to read it. What do you think?

QUESTION #2: I got a rejection letter from a publisher who wrote: "Thank you for your inquiry, but we do not publish in this subject area." Well, here's their chance! I'm thinking about sending my manuscript to them a second time and asking them to be a little more open-minded. Do you think I should?

QUESTION #3: An editor at a different publishing company told me there were "elements" of my proposal that he liked, but he didn't say which ones. Hello! Which ones? I'm tempted to write him back and make him tell me which ones. I think people like assertive people. Do you think I should be more assertive?

QUESTION #4: This could be jumping the gun, but I've been

thinking of ways to promote my book once it gets published. For starters, everyone in my family has promised to buy the book—and it's a big family! Problem: some of the characters in the book are based on my Uncle Earl and his family who we haven't spoken to for almost 10 years. I really don't want to change the names of the people in the book, but maybe I should. What do you think?

As you can see, I really, really, really want to be a published author, like you. Are you doing book tours with your book? I'm totally into the idea of traveling around the country on a book tour. Hey! We could go together! Seriously! Wouldn't that be a hoot!

In conclusion, I think you and I would make a great team. Here's my information so you can get aholt of me. My email is kimball-campbell@yahoo.net, my cell phone number is 123-911-6782, my parent's phone is 123-986-1509, and my current boyfriend's number is 123-688-8333 (although that relationship's a little rocky and he doesn't always give me my messages).

Thanks for reading this. I hope I've captivated—and captured—your interest. Your new friend (and soon-to-be-published author!),

Kitty Kimball-Campbell

P.S. I love the picture of you on the back of your book—you remind me of my grandmother!

RELAX AND UNWIND

My Long-Awaited, Much-Needed Vacation

I love my job, but lately the stress was getting to me. Too much to do. Too little time. Too many deadlines. And then there was my boss. I knew I was losing it when my boss gave me a new project to work on and I just stood there and laughed.

I needed to get out of there.

I needed a vacation.

My travel agent asked me what kind of trip I was looking for. I said I wanted to go somewhere I'd never been. Somewhere with good weather. Somewhere where I could be with happy, relaxed vacationers. I also said I wanted to be pampered, and I *especially* wanted to get an attitude adjustment about my job.

Given the time I could take off from work (very little) and the amount of money I had to spend (very little), she suggested a cruise up the coast of New England into Nova Scotia.

Nova Scotia? I barely knew where Nova Scotia was. I did know that to get to Nova Scotia, we'd be sailing up the coast of New England. That sounded good. New England. New England in the fall. New England in the fall with all the leaves. Leaves that would be changing color. How cool would that be to be able to brag to everyone in the office that I saw the fall leaves in New England?

"It's October," a little voice in my head said. "It could be cold."

"I really need a vacation," a second little voice said.

"True, but it could be cold," the first voice repeated.

I ignored the first little voice and wrote a check to my travel agent.

It was raining in Indianapolis when my flight took off for New York. It rained during the bumpy flight to LaGuardia. It was still raining when I transferred to the ship. I was going to be so glad to get out of the horrible Midwest weather.

The first thing I did aboard ship was what everyone does aboard ship. I went up on deck and watched the ship leave port. People were pointing off the right side of the ship as we passed the Statue of Liberty. I wasn't convinced it was the Statue of Liberty. It might have been, but it was covered in fog.

The second thing I did was the second thing everyone always does—I had dinner in the dining room. I was visiting with the people at my table when the Captain came on the P.A. system. He began by welcoming us aboard. Then he mentioned there was a hurricane in the vicinity, but assured us that everyone on the bridge was going to know where the hurricane was at all times and where the ship was at all times.

Somehow that wasn't very reassuring. What did that even mean?

He added that things might be "a little bumpy" during the night, but that we should "bear with him." What did that mean? How do you "bear with someone" when you're on a ship in a hurricane?

After dinner, I did the third thing everyone does on a cruise—I went to the opening night show in the theatre. Sitting there waiting for the show to begin, I noticed that the heavy velvet curtains on the stage were swaying back and forth. That was interesting. How could something that heavy sway that much? Although the dancers were entertaining, I found myself getting a little queasy.

After the show, on my way back to my room, I tried my best not to collide with my fellow passengers. I walked with my legs as far apart as possible and used the handrails for support. I still wove from side to side and bumped into them.

"Excuse me."

"Sorry."

"I'm new at this."

"Sorry!"

Back in my room, I crawled into bed and drifted off. My last thought was the Captain's promise of better weather.

When I awoke, I noticed that besides rocking from side to side, the ship was now also going up and down. Way up and down. I dressed quickly and went to breakfast. To get to the dining room, I had to descend a flight of stairs. Whoa! That was an interesting sensation— moving in six directions at the same time. Up, down, left, right, backwards, and forward. I enjoy movement, but I prefer moving my body myself rather than having the ship move it for me.

At breakfast, the Captain came on the P.A. system.

"Well, everyone, here's our situation," he started, hesitantly. "We're traveling at twenty-one knots. The hurricane is traveling at twenty-three knots. I thought we could outrun it, but..." and then his voice trailed off.

Say what? You thought you could outrun it? Does that mean we're in FRONT of it? How did *that* happen? Did we *drive* in front of it? I thought you said you were always going to know where the hurricane WAS.

As I tried to stab my hard-boiled egg (that kept moving from one side of the plate to the other), I reminded myself to "bear with it." I still didn't know how to do that. In the Midwest we have tornadoes and I know the drill for that. You take a flashlight and a blanket and make yourself a comfortable place in the basement. But no one was telling us how we should "bear with" being on a ship in a hurricane.

Back in my room, I listened to the Captain's report on the TV monitor. According to the Captain, the sea condition was "moderate." Ha-ha! Moderate.

Being the resourceful person I am, I knew I could find a way to cope with the rocking of the ship. I tried going to the front of the boat, hoping it wouldn't be rocking as much there. It was rocking there.

I went to the middle of the ship. It was rocking there.

I took the elevator up to the top deck to get some fresh air. It didn't help to see the water from the swimming pool crashing in great swells onto the deck.

I tried chewing gum.

I tried eating. Sugar. More sugar. A lot more sugar.

I tried focusing on the horizon. Someone had told me that if you do that you won't get seasick. So, I went to the main lounge and looked out one of the huge windows. At first, the water level was at the bottom of the window. Then it rose to the top. And then it went down to the bottom again. Forget that.

I tried lying down. Sitting up. Standing.

I started repeating the words "I will not get sick. I will not get sick. I will not get sick. I've paid a small fortune for this trip. I will not get sick."

I created a new mantra: "Okay. I may get sick, but it's not going to dampen my vacation."

My fellow passengers grew grumpier by the hour. I could tell they were not bearing with it. "Bear with it!" I called to them in my head. "You're supposed to bear with it!"

Day 3: Breakfast. "Sorry." "Sorry." "Sorry." "Excuse me," we all said as we bumped into each other on our way to the dining room. The waiters, carrying large trays of food over their heads, were weaving so badly they looked like they were drunk.

The good news was there was a pianist playing show tunes. I noticed that the more the boat rocked, the slower he played. And when he sang, he sang very evenly—so the music wouldn't have a distinctive beat.

The Captain came on the P.A. system again.

"Good morning, ladies and gentlemen. Well, the swell right now is much less than I thought it would be."

Say what? What did you think it would be?

We docked at our first port: Sydney. It was cold and rainy. All I saw were umbrellas and yellow rain hats. All I learned about Sydney is that the townspeople own umbrellas and wear yellow rain hats. I bought some maple syrup and returned to the ship to dry off.

Day 4: Halifax. I'd signed up to take an excursion to a "picturesque" fishing village. It was picturesque all right. Picture a huge rainstorm. It was cold, grey, and windy. I learned that the natives called this type of storm a "Nor'easter." It's a cross between a tornado, a typhoon, and a tidal wave. I bought some more maple syrup and returned to the ship to change into dry clothes.

Day 5: St. John, Bay of Fundy. The Captain came on the P.A. system and told us—with great gusto—to look out the window at the beautiful sunny day. Then he went back to bed. The sunshine lasted about five minutes. That was the last we heard from the Captain. Even he gave up on this cruise.

As we lined up to go ashore for our excursion, the second-in-command came on the P.A. system to report that the city of St. John had closed its port due to high winds. We wouldn't be able to dock there. We were going to have to stay on board ship. Oh, and by the way, don't go out on deck until the winds died down. He invited us to join him in the main lounge for a game of Bingo.

According to the TV monitor in my room, the seas were now deemed to be "rough." No shit, Sherlock. Tomorrow was supposed to be better.

I went to Bingo. Bingo is a really stupid game.

It was time for me to go to my "happy place." I folded a blanket and sat cross-legged on it on the floor. I began deep breathing. Deep breath in. Deep breath out. The ship rocked. I tipped to the right and conked my head against the door. I repositioned myself. The ship rocked again. This time I tipped to the left and hit my head on the bed. So much for going to my happy place.

I checked the revised list of activities for the day. There was going to be a yoga class at two o'clock. Yoga is quiet and relaxing. I decided to go to the class.

Arriving at the fitness room, I took a purple yoga mat and unrolled it on the floor. Several people were already stretched out, relaxing, so I lay down and began relaxing, too. Yes. This might just get me to my happy place.

Shortly, the eighteen-year-old, instructor (an Olympic gymnast) entered the room with loud hip hop music blaring from her boom box. She invited us to get on our feet to get our heart rates going. Oh-Kay. That wasn't the way we started yoga class back home, but maybe they start yoga a little differently on a cruise.

The music increased in volume, intensity, and speed. After we did some jumping jacks, she had us touch our knees to our elbows. Huh? I raised my hand.

"Excuse me," I said. "Is this the yoga class?"

"No. This is the cardio class."

Wonderful. Deciding I didn't want to break an arm and a leg (because even the coast guard wouldn't have come to get me in this weather) I returned my mat to the bin and excused myself.

I checked the revised list of activities again. There was going to be a movie in the theatre. I could use a good movie. Now, most of the passengers on board (who, remember, weren't bearing with it any better than I was) were in their seventies and eighties. We needed a good Fred Astaire movie. Instead, we got a movie about a superhero with robot jet fighters shooting a giant space octopus.

I returned to my room ("Sorry." "Sorry." "Sorry." "Excuse me."), called room service and had them bring me one of every dessert they had.

On the last night of the cruise, the activities director jumped up onstage and cried: "Are you having a good time?" The audience remained mute. What cruise had he been on all week? Instead of taking our silence as a cue, the silly man asked his question again, even louder. "Are you having a good time?" A few people mumbled "yes." They were probably the BINGO winners.

The final show was a troupe of acrobats. Picture this: you're in a theatre, the boat is rocking, you look up, and there's a guy hooked to two bungee cords, coming straight down at your head. He does a somersault, and quickly ascends back to the ceiling. Over and over. Onstage, his fellow acrobats are swinging from one side of the stage to the other holding onto ropes and hula hoops. Other acrobats are doing cartwheels. There was constant movement. Whoever designed the show did not design it for a ship in a hurricane.

To sum things up, it rained for seven straight days, I saw no fall leaves, and I gained ten pounds.

I will admit— I *did* have a major attitude adjustment. I couldn't wait to get back to work.

Should've Just Sent a Present

This spring, I was invited to a wedding in Phoenix.

I'd never been to Phoenix, so I decided to go. I needed a trip. It would be fun.

I packed my best wedding guest outfit—a pair of silky black slacks and a grey (sort-of-see-through) sparkly grey top with three-quarter length sleeves. Since you could see through the grey top, I had a grey T-shirt to wear underneath. I also packed my black heels and black nylons.

Got my ticket. Flew to Phoenix. Landed in Phoenix.

Stepped outside the airport. OMG. Bright lights! Bright lights! What was it—sunshine? We don't have sunshine in Indiana. And when we do, the clouds have enough sense to cover it up.

I fished around in my bag and found my sunglasses. They didn't help. And it was hot. The temperature gauge on the dashboard of my rental car reported ninety-five degrees, and that's having been in a cool, breezy parking garage.

I pulled out on I-17 and discovered that "Phoenix" is an ancient Greek word for "one hell of a lot of traffic." There were six lanes of cars—all going seventy miles per hour—and none of us could see where we were going because we were all blinded by the sun. There were overpasses and underpasses. And overpasses that went over the overpasses and underpasses.

My body cried out for water.

Hang on, I answered my body. We'll be at the rehearsal shortly. Your body temperature will return to normal. You'll be out of the sun. And I'm sure they'll have water.

By some miracle, about forty-five minutes later, I found the wedding rehearsal. My friends were standing outside a beautiful expensive-looking resort. Were they outside waiting for me?

"I made it! We can go in," I said.

"In where?"

"Inside. To rehearse."

"Oh. The rehearsal's going to be outside."

"Because...?"

"Because the wedding's going to be outside." They pointed to the rows of white folding chairs on the front lawn. No trees. No shade. An aisle down the middle for the bride. Surely that wasn't for our wedding.

I laughed. "Be serious."

"We're serious."

There went my black heels, black nylons, black slacks, grey top, and grey T-shirt.

"Well, it cools off in the evening, doesn't it?" I said, hopefully.

"A little. But the wedding's at two-thirty."

"Come on," I laughed. "Get serious."

"We're serious."

Well, at least we won't be facing the sun, I said it to myself. I looked up. Where was the sun? Wait. There was the sun. We were going to be facing the sun.

"Be sure to bring water," my friends said. "It's supposed to be one hundred and two tomorrow."

The rehearsal was blessedly short. After the rehearsal, I found a drugstore and bought sunscreen and a case of bottled water. Then I checked into my hotel, and searched through my suitcase to try to find something I could wear to the wedding. This caused me to wonder. How do women in Phoenix shop for their clothes? In Indiana, we dress in layers, or we wear wool. We wear a lot of wool. It occurred to me that in Phoenix, women must shop for their clothes by weight.

"What are you shopping for?" the saleslady would say.

"A dress to wear to a wedding."

"Oh. Would you like a one-pound dress?"

"No, the wedding's going to be outside. I'd like just a half-pound dress."

Next day. Wedding. One hundred and two degrees, facing the sun. Someone once told me dry heat wasn't as bad as humid heat. Ha-ha! They should buy the Brooklyn Bridge.

The bride was in a long white dress. The groom, best men, and father of the bride were all in black tuxedos. Everyone was wearing sunglasses. We looked like we were filming a movie about the mob.

Instead of taking one of the little bottles of water with me, I carried a half gallon jug and drank directly from the rim. After each swig, I'd pour some water into my hands and splash my face. Then, I'd apply sunscreen to my arms and legs. None of that behavior made me stand out. I did stand out, though, because I was the only person there without a tattoo.

Every city has its own song. Chicago has "Chicago." New York has "New York, New York, It's a Wonderful Town." San Francisco has "I Left my Heart in San Francisco." I decided the song for Phoenix should be "Oh, God, I'm Dying" from *Godspell*.

Now, this was a Catholic wedding. Catholics have really long weddings. The wedding party stood, facing the sun, the entire time. This included the three bridesmaids, the three groomsmen, and both sets of parents. In the beginning, the men were stoic, but eventually they started flapping the sides of their jackets like they were trying to take off. The bridesmaids fanned themselves with their hands. One of the bridesmaids started swaying back and forth, so another bridesmaid walked her over to a chair. That's when the fleas came out and started biting our ankles. The women in the bridal party tried to balance on one of their high-heeled platform shoes and use the toe of the other shoe to scratch the backs of their legs.

The priest suffered the most in the heat with his long garments and headgear. It didn't help that English was his second language. For whatever reason, he conducted the service in English which meant that there were long pauses when he was trying to think of the right word. Bless his heart. He stumbled over his choice of words. Sometimes he got into loops of words where he repeated himself over and over. Either that's part of a Catholic service, or the heat was getting to him. Once, he called the groom by the wrong name. Twice, he called the bride by the wrong name. At one point he got confused and asked which one was which. After about an hour, he threw up his hands and switched over to Spanish. A member of the bridal party took the microphone and interpreted the rest of the ceremony into English.

The wedding lasted an hour and twenty minutes. Since I'm prone to exaggeration, I checked with the guy sitting next to me.

"Was that an hour and fifteen minutes?"

He checked his watch. "No, it was an hour and twenty."

I love Catholics, but we Methodists would have had everyone in and out of there in ten.

Actually, the bride was beautiful. The groom was handsome. Both sets of parents were happy. The guests were happy. I got happy after I got to the reception and had a couple of glasses of wine. I took my shoes off, like everyone else, and danced the night away.

But the next time someone invites me to their wedding, I'm going to read the invitation more carefully. And if it's an outdoor wedding in Phoenix, I'm going to send a present ... and my regrets.

Las Vegas through the Eyes of a Midwesterner

Sam and I wanted to take a trip somewhere that would be different from Indiana, so we decided to go to Las Vegas. We don't gamble, drink, or stay up late, but we thought it might be fun to see what we were missing.

It *was* fun, and the trip *did* confirm that Las Vegas is different from Indiana. Here's Las Vegas from a Midwesterner's point of view.

Arriving in Vegas: Starting with our ride on the shuttle from the airport to our hotel, everything was bigger, faster, taller, flashier, and more outlandish than we had imagined. The hotel we stayed at was humongous. It had 4,400 rooms. They bragged you could put nine 747's (without any of them touching) in its atrium. Before I left on vacation, a friend told me I'd be doing a lot of walking. She'd recently visited Vegas and said it took her forty-five minutes to find where she was going.

"You mean to walk from one end of the strip to the other?" I asked.

"No. To walk from one end of a hotel to the other." She was right.

Checking Into the Hotel: From the moment we entered the hotel, Sam started pointing to things. "Look there!" "Wow!" "Look at that!" An attractive lady with a name tag immediately came up to us.

"How long will you be staying in Vegas?" she smiled.

"Four days."

"Wonderful!" she said, delightedly. "We have a special offer you might be interested in." She walked us over to another attractive lady behind a counter who was equally as excited and happy to meet us.

"You can help us out," she began. "While you're here, there are a number of things you can get discounts on. For fifty dollars ... " She talked so quickly we couldn't understand what she was saying.

"Start over," we said.

"You give us fifty dollars cash..." she began again.

"Wait. You want *us* to give *you* fifty dollars cash?"

"Yes, and here's what you get..."

"You're serious? You want *us* to give *you* fifty dollars?"

She said "yes" again.

"We're not interested." I pulled Sam away.

She frowned. We'd obviously ruined her day. And she obviously thought we'd ruined ours, as well.

I took Sam aside and told him to stop pointing. It was drawing attention to us. Although maybe it wasn't just the pointing. Maybe it was the old-fashioned camera he wore around his neck and the yellow plastic "M and M" purse from Wal-Mart I had over my shoulder.

On our way to our room, another hotel employee stopped us and smiled: "How long are you going to be in Vegas?"

Thinking I could outsmart her, I replied: "Five minutes."

"Wonderful! We have a special deal for you. Come on over to this desk ..."

When she turned to walk us over, we ducked behind a slot machine. After that, we avoided people with name tags.

Things I Would Change About the Hotels: I would add more signs and more exits. I'm sure there were exits, but they weren't marked. To get anywhere in any of the hotels, you have to pass through the casinos, which are smoky. I'm not a big fan of smoke. So, when we had to walk through a casino, I'd take Sam's hand, close my eyes, and let him lead me through the smoke. Every so often I'd open my eyes.

And see a scantily-clad young woman milling about.

I'd close them. A minute later, I'd open them again.

I'd see another scantily-clad young woman milling about.

I'd close them again.

That kept happening. Maybe that's why Sam took so long getting us out of there.

Personally, I think the front desk should give their guests a Boy Scout mountaineering map and compass when they check in. Sam and I were in our hotel for four days and never did figure out how to get back and forth to our room. We either wandered around like Moses in the desert, or we had to ask someone. When we could, we tried to find a maintenance worker. One time I stood back and watched Sam ask for directions. The employee gestured for a while with his right hand. Then for a while with his left. Then he pointed up (that must have indicated an elevator). Sam thanked him and came over to where I was standing.

"So where do we go?"

"I have no idea."

My Motherly Instinct: While I was there, I worried about the people at the slot machines. Some of them looked pasty, bleary-eyed, and out-of-it. I felt a strong urge to approach them.

"Hey—I'm going to the library. Can I pick you up a book?"

"Does your mother know how long you've been here?"

"Oh, *this* is your mother?"

"Did you both have your nine servings of fruits and vegetables today?"

"Do you mind if I ask—are you drinking enough water? You know, the rule-of-thumb is to drink an eight-ounce glass of water after you drink a glass of something else. Have you been doing that?"

"How about this section of players over here ... why don't you all stand up and we'll do some yoga stretches together. How many of you can do the downward dog?"

I just wanted to take them out to get some sunshine.

Most Daring Thing I Did in Vegas: I did something I never would have done back in Indiana. I tried the massage chair on the second floor of Harrah's (right outside the theatre we were waiting to go in). I put a dollar in the slot on the side of the machine, and for three minutes, rollers in the back of the chair ran up and down my spine. It felt great! I relaxed. I closed my eyes. "You need to try this, Sam," I moaned. When it was over, I opened my eyes and saw that everybody waiting in line for the theatre had been watching me.

What was REALLY great about it is that now I have a story to tell when I get home. When I get home, people are going to ask: "Did you go on the zip line?" "Did you see David Copperfield?" "Did you go up in the Stratosphere?" "Did you eat at Mucho Macho?" Those are the things *they* did when they visited Vegas, and they're going to try to make it sound like what *they* did was better than what Sam and I did. This time I'll have a comeback. I'll be able to say (coyly): "Did *you* try the massage chair at Harrah's?"

Another Neat Thing: One day we took the double Decker bus and got off at the Mob Museum. It's housed in a renovated old post office building with marble floors and stair cases. There are three floors. The displays are awesome. They have movies and videos, a facsimile of an early electric chair, a courtroom, and a room where you can try your hand at shooting a gun at a bad guy. Really interesting and really well done.

The Shows: Were amazing! Sam wanted to see *The Blue Man Group*, which we did, and I wanted to see *Legends*, a show with impersonators of famous singers. They had Dean Martin, Tom Jones, Elvis, Celine Dion, and Lady Gaga (Lady Gaga? With Dean Martin? That was kind of bizarre.) While singing "I Can't Help Falling in Love with You," the Elvis impersonator came to the edge of the stage, squatted down, and motioned me to come over. When I did, he kissed me on the cheek. It was almost as good as the massage chair.

I'm not sure why he picked me. Maybe it was my yellow, plastic "M and M" purse from Wal-Mart.

My Most Embarrassing Moment: The tour guide on our double Decker bus told us there are strict rules in Las Vegas for watering your lawn. She explained that to save water, some of the hotels use artificial grass, and that sometimes you could see people cleaning it with a vacuum or a broom.

I chimed in, trying to sound as knowledgeable and superior as I could: "That's better than in Phoenix. In Phoenix, they have front yards made of GRAVEL."

The tour guide looked at me and said: "*I* have a front yard made of gravel."

Oh. Never mind.

Coming Home: We had as much fun flying on Southwest as we did in Vegas. Their flight attendants sang songs and made even their directions sound funny. Here are some of the things they said:

"The flight attendants are going to come through the cabin to make sure your seat belts are fastened and that your socks match."

"Smoking is permitted outside, on the wings of the plane. The movie you'll be seeing is 'Gone with the Wind.'"

"Should you need oxygen, put your own mask on first, then your favorite child's, and work your way down to your husband."

"Thank you for flying from Las Vegas to Indianapolis with us. This is a continuing flight to Kansas City. If you are staying on the plane and going to Kansas City ... Dude, you need a new travel agent."

Things I Enjoyed Coming Home to: Lawns made out of green grass. Shade trees. Lights that stay on rather than flash on and off. The smell of manure rather than the smell of cigarette smoke. People who go to bed early. Finding the way to my bedroom without having to ask for directions. Being able to wear my tennis shoes and carry my yellow plastic purse without having to worry about whether or not I fit in.

What I Miss About Las Vegas: The automatic paper towel dispensers. My first day back at work, I was in the ladies' room trying to get a paper towel by moving my hand back and forth in front of the dispenser. Nothing happened.

My boss came in and reminded me:

"Smack it."

A Secret about Myself

A Poemette
By
Sara Jane Coffman

When I was growing up
My mother watched the Lawrence Welk show.
I swore I never would.
But now,
Sometimes
Late at night
When I'm all alone
I watch it, too.
And I'm starting to like it.

Especially when he does the polka.

CPSIA information can be obtained at www.ICGtesting.com
Printed in the USA
BVOW071409170313

315677BV00001B/14/P